With a starting point on July 14, 2021, when the Centre national de littérature hosted Pierre Joris' 75th birthday celebration, *Always the Many, Never the One* builds upon the initial interview by Florent Toniello that took place that day to go deeper into a major Luxembourg-American poet's reflections on literature, philosophy, and life. Throughout this book Joris develops a core concept of his thinking and writing, "in-betweenness," using both literary examples & life anecdotes, some never shared in Joris's vast bibliography so far.

The form is representative of the "in-between" concept: while it comprises the initial oral interview at the CNL plus seven subsequent interviews conducted virtually, the whole text was reworked in order to complete the thoughts and add necessary or relevant references, thus transforming it also into a literary essay; but the interview-tone remains, making for lively & stimulating reading. Beyond discussing the "in-betweenness" concept, Joris shares his views on a range of subjects related to poetry, translation, music and the arts while linking his work to the theoretical thinking and craft of leading past and present philosophers and writers/poets, in a dazzling literary world tour-de-force.

To complement this first (and major) part of the book, two "bonuses" follow: a reprint of the interview Joris gave for a recent book by Florent Toniello, *Mélusine au gasoil* (in line with Contra Mundum's multilingual ethos, this is provided in the original French version), and the speech Joris gave at the award ceremony for the Batty Weber prize, to also make this talk-essay available to a wider audience.

PRAISE FOR *ALWAYS THE MANY, NEVER THE ONE*

Pierre Joris is phenomenal, a rare (unprecedented?) combination of serendipity and gumption. He's a hydra-headed omnivore, eyeing the delightful & the grim with equal savvy. These conversations are at once a deft feather touch to the heart & a blistering grimace in the face of the constant darkening of our time. Listen in — and as the saying goes, *stay tuned*. — JED RASULA

This generous and engaging book is an album of conversations, including Pierre Joris's speech in his first country, Luxembourg ("a portable small country"), upon winning its major literary prize. Joris (with Florent Toniello) assembles witty, ranging, informed, and passionate insights on the vectors of contemporary poetics. From translation to nomadism, from "the between" to the scintillation of borders, from his critique of toxic gender/race myths to lively riffs on genre (particularly epic & long poem), Joris's convictions are telling, & his aphorisms are generative. *Always the Many, Never the One* is a defining overview of a distinctive poetic career. — RACHEL BLAU DUPLESSIS

The duet, lush with resonance and reference, has become a beautiful habit for Pierre Joris. His interviews let you see so far outside that coming around again, but off, is easy. The resulting spiral is a new curriculum & in this "riot of air" it's almost like we know all that he knows. — FRED MOTEN

A fascinating collection of conversations that run the gamut from poetry to film, music, philosophy, critical theory, and more. With an encyclopedic knowledge, profound understanding, and sparkling wit, Joris illuminates and elucidates upon Olson, Duncan, Brakhage, Schneeman, Enheduanna, Boulez, Cage, Coltrane, Kurosawa, Godard, Karl May, Ed Dorn, Rothenberg, Ibn Tarafa, Rimbaud, Assia Djebar, Edouard Glissant, Zukofsky, Giordano Bruno, and the art of translating Burroughs, Kerouac, Celan and more. Freewheeling & spontaneous, these are immensely invigorating exchanges between two kindred spirits. — JOHN ZORN

The conversations gathered here, like Joris's poems & writings over-all, bring a whole world into view, many worlds in fact, in the best tradition of a new American and new World poetry as it has come to him in his lifetime and ours. And like the poetry itself, it is the voice, always, of a man talking & self-exploring, with a casualness of tone amid a loaded plethora of knowledges and day-by-day observations & protocols: the presence too of a comic temperament that's as serious as it gets — from a master of multiple languages and of language-secrets that he freely shares with us. Much to our enlightenment and downright pleasure.
— JEROME ROTHENBERG, Encinitas, California, 2022

*Always the Many
Never the One*

※

Pierre Joris

Also by Pierre Joris

POETRY

Fox-trails, -tails, & -trots (Poems & Proses) (Black Fountain Press, 2020)
The Book of U / Le Livre des cormorans (avec Nicole Peyrafitte) (Éditions Simoncini, 2017)
Canto Diurno (French Selected; Le Castor astral 2017)
An American Suite (Inpatient Press, 2016)
Gulf Od Vraku K Pohromé (Czech translation; Prague, 2016)
Barzakh (Poems 2000–2012) (Black Widow Press, 2014)
Mawqif: Poemas y ensayos (Mexico D.F.: La Otra, 2014). Spanish Translation
Meditations on the Stations of Mansur al-Hallaj (Chax Press, 2013)
The Gulf (Between You & Me) (The Crossing, 2013)
learn the shadow (unit 4 art, 2012)
Canto Diurno #4: The Tang Extending from the Blade (ebook; 2010)
Aljibar & Aljibar II (Éditions PHI, 2007; 2008)
Routes, not Roots (Audio CD, 2007)
Meditations on the Stations of Mansur Al-Hallaj 1–20 (Chax Press, 2006)
The Rothenberg Variations (Wild Honey Press, 2004)
Fin de siècle-Phantombild; Ausgewählte Gedichte 1974–2000 (PHI, 2004)
Permanent Diaspora (Duration Press, 2003)
Poasis: Selected Poems 1986–1999 (Wesleyan U.P., 2001)
h.j.r. (Otherwind Press, 1999)
out/takes (Backwoods Broadsides, 1999)
La Dernière Traversée de la Manche (PHI, 1995)
Winnetou Old (Meow Press, 1994)
Turbulence (St. Lazaire Press, 1991)
The Irritation Ditch (Parentheses Writing Series, 1991)
Janus (St. Lazaire Press, 1988)
Breccia: Selected Poems 1972–1986 (PHI, 1987)
Net/Work (Spanner Books, 1983)

The Book of Luap Nalec (Ta'wil Books, 1982)
make it up like say (Arc Publications, 1982)
Tracing (Arc Publications, 1982)
The Broken Glass (Pig Press, 1980)
Old Dog High Q (Writers Forum, 1980)
Body Count (Twisted Wrist, 1979)
The Tassili Connection (Ta'wil Books, 1978)
Tanith Flies (Ta'wil Books, 1978)
Hearth-Work (Hatch Books, 1977)
Antlers I–XI (New London Pride, 1975)
A Single-minded Bestiary (Privately Printed, 1974)
Trance/Mutations (1972)
The Fifth Season (Strange Faeces Press, 1971)

PROSE

Arabia (not so) Deserta — Essays on Maghrebi & Mashreqi Writing & Culture (Spuyten Duyvil, 2019)
Adonis & Pierre Joris, *Conversations in the Pyrenees* (Contra Mundum, 2019; bilingual edition)
The Agony of I.B. (Theater; Éditions PHI, 2016)
Justifying the Margins (Salt, 2009)
A Nomad Poetics (Wesleyan U.P., 2003)
Global Interference (Liberation Press, 1981)
The Book of Demons (with Victoria Hyatt, as Joseph W. Charles) (Simon & Schuster, 1975)
The Entropy Caper (radio play; 1973)
Another Journey (Privately Printed, 1972)

Always the Many, Never the One

Conversations In-between Mersch
& Elsewhere

Always the Many, Never the One

Conversations In-between Mersch & Elsewhere

Pierre Joris with Florent Toniello

Contra Mundum Press   New York · London · Melbourne

Always the Many, Never the One: Conversations In-between Mersch & Elsewhere © 2022 Pierre Joris and Florent Toniello

First Contra Mundum Press Edition 2022.

All Rights Reserved under International & Pan-American Copyright Conventions. No part of this book may be reproduced in any form or by any electronic means, including information storage and retrieval systems, without permission in writing from the publisher, except by a reviewer who may quote brief passages in a review.

Library of Congress Cataloguing-in-Publication Data

Joris, Pierre, 1946– and Toniello, Florent, 1972–

Always the Many, Never the One: Conversations In-between Mersch & Elsewhere / Pierre Joris & Florent Toniello

—1st Contra Mundum Press Edition 156 pp., 6 x 9 in.

ISBN 9781940625584

I. Joris, Pierre, and Toniello, Florent.
II. Title.

2022943903

With the support of Kultur|lx Arts Council Luxembourg

Table of Contents

PREFACE: Why, when, & how? (Florent Toniello)	2
1ST CONVERSATION	5
2ND CONVERSATION	17
3RD CONVERSATION	29
4TH CONVERSATION	41
5TH CONVERSATION	57
6TH CONVERSATION	66
7TH CONVERSATION	77
8TH CONVERSATION	90
Entretien avec Pierre Joris pour *Mélusine au gasoil*	107
Batty Weber Award Speech	110

Always the Many, Never the One

PREFACE

Why, when, & how?

During October 2017, Pierre Joris was in Luxembourg with his wife Nicole Peyrafitte for their exhibition *Domopoetic Works* at the Galerie Simoncini. I had started reporting on Joris & Peyrafitte's work at the beginning of my work as a journalist, in 2015; it was therefore only natural that I would meet Joris & exchange a few words, in order to craft an article on the exhibition & its opening performance. But, this time, something special came up. In the summer, Joris had been conducting a series of conversations with Syrian poet Adonis that would result in the book *Conversations in the Pyrenees*.[1] He had enjoyed this experience so much that he was thinking of working on a conversation book of his own: tucked in between essay & interview, in between oral & written, such a book would represent, according to him, a new & enjoyable genre to blend poetry, life anecdotes, & theoretical thoughts. And I was to be his partner to make this happen.

That Joris asked me to work with him on this project was at first puzzling, if not intimidating. After all, why would an award-winning long-time practitioner of poetry trust a former information technology manager only recently turned proofreader, journalist, & poet to perform a good enough job on such an important book to him? To which I know Joris would answer, in his usual manner, "Why not?" I suspect that, in his mind, the keen poetry reader I am, combined with interviewing skills & my lack of an academic background in literature, would help drive the book to the in-between he consistently strives for.

1. Adonis & Pierre Joris, *Conversations in the Pyrénées* (Contra Mundum Press, 2018).

It took a while, however, before we started working concretely on the project — although it remained part of our subsequent conversations. The year 2021 gave us a push that could not be resisted: first, Joris was finally allowed to travel to Luxembourg to receive the Batty Weber Prize awarded to him in 2020, a year shaken up by the coronavirus crisis; second, he turned 75 on July 14th. The Luxembourg National Literature Archive (Centre national de littérature) not only hosted the award ceremony, but a few days later also helped set up a more intimist, yet public, birthday celebration on its premises in Mersch. Joris & I decided that the first part thereof would be an interview of him by me, to kickstart our series of talks that would become a book. It was followed by seven others, this time online.

Improvisation plays an important part in Joris's work. That is why I prepared this whole series by digging deep into his books (poetry, translations, & essays alike, as well as essays on his work) but never shared questions upfront. He would discover them during our interview sessions, each one preceded by a preliminary talk in order to discuss more mundane matters. After each session, I would transcribe it as faithfully as possible & send the text to him, which he would in turn revise & expand or clarify. That is why this book oscillates between oral & written style, something that we did not want to remove in order to preserve both the spontaneity of speech as well as the depth of written language. That is also why we did not reorder questions or answers too much: there is a flow in this entire work that comes from our choice of a carefully led improvisation. Some themes return regularly, some questions are "queered," some anecdotes alluded to may come in another book — it is a living, not too polished, yet constructed work you are about to read. An in-between. But this in-between can also be seen as an "entre-tien": Joris & I usually talk in French (a remainder of my shyness to use his native Luxembourgish, an acquired language to me, back in 2015), yet conversations were held in English, the language he chose decades ago to be his writing language.

Hours after Joris's birthday celebration on July 14, 2021, severe flooding affected the building of the National Literature Archive, whose cellar was under several meters of water for many days. This dramatic episode led me to write a relatively long poem, finally published in early 2022 in a series of books for which the publisher requests an interview between the author & a person of their choice.[2] It was obvious to me that I had to ask Joris. This additional interview, in French, is therefore also included in this book, because it shares the same starting point as the eight conversations that precede it. Because of the link with the Batty Weber Prize ceremony, this book also features the speech Pierre gave on this occasion, originally published as a booklet by the Centre national de littérature.

It is now time to read our conversations & listen to what *Pierre Joris* has to share. May you feel comfortable in our *entre-tien*, our *in-between*!

FT

---

2. Florent Toniello, *Mélusine au gasoil* (Facteur Galop, 2022).

1st Conversation[3]

July 14, 2021

FLORENT TONIELLO: *At one point, in* Conversations in the Pyrénées *with Adonis, you talk about including down-to-earth subjects, that is social & environmental ones in poems, & this gets cut somehow. I'd like to know more about that. How does this relate to the work of the poet?*

PIERRE JORIS: During the reading after our interview I will read a poem that outlines the role of the poet in three verses.[4] I'll be much broader now. My ideas about this come from meetings with people & books: coming to America — I had already been seduced by the Beats & their very public jazz-inflected poetry & prose — meant leaving Europe & its way-too-narrow lyric-poetry scene. I was lucky enough to immediately run into poets such as Robert Kelly, who introduced me to the work of Charles Olson, Robert Duncan, & the other Black Mountain people. Kelly has a beautiful essay where he calls the poet "a scientist of the whole."[5] He — but others too, such as Muriel Rukeyser, who also brought science into poetry, insisting that they were complementary ways of knowing

---

3. This first interview took place in the Centre national de littérature in Mersch, during a public celebration of Joris' 75th birthday. Fellow writers guests were the writers Nico Helminger, Alice Notley, & Habib Tengour, as well as Nicole Peyrafitte, who moderated the reading session following the interview. Both interviewer and interviewee would like to express their deepest thanks to all staff at the CNL for this memorable evening, on the eve of a tragic flooding that severely affected the building.
4. The Poet's Job // Pick up everything that shines / Discard the gold // Keep the light.
5. *A Voice Full of Cities. The Collected Essays of Robert Kelly*, ed. by Pierre Joris & Peter Cockelbergh (CMP 2014) 103.

the world — opened a new space for the poem: the poem as an open field, to use the Olson/Duncan terminology, into which any kind of information can come. So it's the job of the poet to organize the various multi-sourced information she feels relevant so as to create a poem on the page. And that can be her dailiness, whatever happens in the morning as the poet gets up. There the lingering dreams of the fading night can meet up with the milk delivery man & cart & start the work off, & from there you can get into the garden, & there are those flowers, & they are not just flowers, like metaphors, they are specific kinds of flowers, & they're useful for this & that, medicinally, herbalistically, eco-logically... That's the way. Then you open a book, maybe check some background info on that flower, or get an email from a friend, & that too can enter the poem. *Voilà!* What I discovered was that anything & everything can & should in some way enter the poem & in the process help create a more open, a wider structure. Robert Duncan's sense of the poem as "grand collage" is still useful to me, & I love the long works (not "epic" — at least not in that Western-Civ very young male-warrior mode, which is not useful to think with or through in our own day & age, even if we probably have as much if not more carnage than in the days of the Trojan War), the long works of a range of my contemporaries who rather than glorifying military success, try to propose non-bellicose ways & means of understanding & living on this endangered planet.

The concept of anything entering the poem is quite interesting, because in the anthology of Luxembourgish poets that was just published in France by Jean Portante, Lignes de partage, *there's this poem by you where you even write about a baseball game. It's a poem for Robert Kelly's birthday. Now, social & environmental subjects, is that because you feel a certain responsibility to bring these to public attention?*

Well, yes, & unless you only look back & take poetry as this navel-gazing occasion, the world is bigger & the world is in trouble. In truth, we're up shit's creek without a paddle. So what we need to do as poets is to deal with that predicament. Of course, we can also do small funny things, or write love poems to our lovers, there too everything & anything can come into the poem, but unless we address what is going down in the world, what's the point? The ecological is obviously core to what our contemporaneity is all about. It's not necessarily easy to find ways to do this. A so-called "ecopoetics" can also very quickly become relatively academic or over-romantically feely-feely, feely-touchy "nature-poetry." That's not what we want — because that risks too much repetition, or restating what we already know, & for me the successful poem (or simply any successful piece of writing) is the one that tells you (the reader, or me, the writer) something we didn't yet know. Writing has to be explorative, has to be discovery.

You mention baseball in my poem for Robert Kelly: so yes, there you have a so-called "occasional" poem, a birthday poem, & the baseball reference has at least a double sense: Robert & I love that New York baseball team, the Mets, & love talking about them when we get around a table — or even just on the phone. But it is wider than that: it is also a thank you note to Robert. When I got to Bard College in 1967, I asked him what was the best way to improve my spoken & written English — which was still a bit stilted & British because acquired in a Luxembourg high school from an Oxford-educated teacher, even if American movies & meetings with G.I.s & listening to early rock had also sharpened my appetite for the US version of English — as I wanted to be a poet in this language, & he told me to listen to baseball radio broadcasts as that was one of, if not the richest & most diverse ways in which the American language was used orally. I did & it was a true initiation into American culture.

Now, about the target audience: who would you say you want to touch?

Listen, a target is something you shoot at. I don't shoot at anybody, so in that sense I don't have a target audience. I mean, of course, I'd love everybody to read me, but I'm a realist. 246, or at best 863 people, roughly, on average, something of that order for a book of poems? Maybe a few more at some point. But the important thing is for the work to be there & available. If it is needed, it will be picked up. I have that kind of confidence that people, young people — & I've seen that during the years I was teaching — are looking for things & will find what they need (& for me teaching is exactly that: not imparting knowledge you have & they don't, but laying out techniques enabling both the students & you to find out things you didn't know but need to know or didn't even know you needed).

In the introduction to An American Suite, *Tamas Panitz recalls that Robert Kelly once answered a question from an audience member that said "Where would you put [classify] Pierre Joris's poetry today?" by saying: "In the hands of any reader or to-be reader of poetry." I think that's very consistent with what you mentioned. Now, how do you reach out to would-be readers? Because you say that it's available out there, but, of course, you do more: you perform, for example.*

Indeed, there isn't just one audience, there's at least two: those who buy books to read in the traditional silence of their rooms & those who come to readings & performances. Obviously, they overlap to some extent, & reinforce each other to some extent too, but that return to the oral performance of poetry & the integration of poetry/text/language, whatever you want to call it, into performance art has expanded the visibility & the enjoy-ability of poetry.

Nicole Peyrafitte & I do a lot of performance work together, often calling on musicians to contribute — we both love to perform with a variety of musicians & musical takes, from jazz to more classical or more electronic incarnations of that sound-language called music. You've witnessed both in Luxembourg, including the latest one with your son Colin on digital piano! We also often include videos & moving images. Both our sons are in movies: obviously, they have a bigger built-in audience. With me in poetry, & Nicole as artist & performer, our audience is of course different from a movie audience.

NICOLE PEYRAFITTE: *Although today we are live on Facebook.*

How many people are following the feed?

A million & a half!

Wonderful, now it's time to recite some poems!

Nicole & I have a fight about this, actually. She calls me an old whore, because I have accepted everybody on Facebook & now I have 5,000 "friends."

There's also another way to possibly widen the audience; it would be to go beyond poetry. It's also in the book with Adonis: you talk about the novel. I know your dislike for this genre, but you don't develop it in that conversation. Can you speak a bit more about that?

I can develop it fully in four words: *the novel is dead.* That's something I learned very young. It seemed to me that the novel was very much a 19th-century genre. There is some writing with justified margins, which is very good & that I love reading. [*Looks at Nico Helminger in the audience.*] Nico does this, for example.

This was not rehearsed!

It's writing of the intensity of poetry but with justified margins, that's all. David Antin once quipped that prose was just a special kind of visual or concrete poetry with the limiting formal requirements of justified left & right margins (suggesting that "prose" as we know it is a development of technology & in its modern form only comes into existence with the invention of the printing press). The novel as the literary genre that proposes imagined "characters" whose "character" & actions develop after some very serious event or insight, & that the writer invents, understands & moves about, shadowing them like that white-bearded male Judeo-Christian god is supposed to shadow his "children," well... The thing is, if you walk around a city, any city, you can meet people who are way more interesting than anything you could "invent" as a character. So why invent characters? For me at least, this was never interesting. This may just be my own prejudice — as much writing I like gets characterized as "novel" or "roman" (as probably more commercially viable *appellations contrôlées* than "text" or "poem" would be), from Kafka to Gertrude Stein to Samuel Beckett or Maurice Blanchot, *und so weiter*. Writing a poem, gathering information that clashes & surprises when I juxtapose it, wow, that's way more interesting. Because it can surprise & thus change *me*. So the traditional, 19C "novel" is not a genre that interests me. Now maybe that's so simply because I'm incapable of writing one. I did try once, in a hotel in Paris, over a 48-hour period, on amphetamine, when a new girlfriend after a very intense affair over a few days left me for her fiancé who had arrived from Stockholm. They were on the 6th floor, & I was in a room on the 3rd floor, very desperate. So I took all the amphetamines I could find & for three days typed away. I had 120 pages when I was done. I never published it. It was bad. Bad, fake Kerouac — I was probably as awed by his novel *Tristessa*, written in 24 or 48 hours sitting on the john, high on whatever, in a junkie's pad in Mexico City, as I was by my brief love affair.

NICOLE PEYRAFITTE: *When was this?*

1971 or 1972.

It sounds like an obsession, because the first thing — or almost the first thing — you ever said to me, during our first interview for my newspaper, was: "The novel is dead." I do remember that very well. And yet, in Justifying the Margins, *you feature essays about Arabic writers that you praise for their novels, because they write in French, conveying with the language of the oppressor what they have to express. Is that the exception for you, the margins justified?*

Absolutely. When I went to Paris, I went to medical school, dropped out in my second year, & decided to become a writer in English because the poetry in this language was the most alive, interesting, honest, groundbreaking (add whatever adjective you want!) I had come across. Not that some prose wasn't great: I already mentioned Kerouac whose "spontaneous jazz-bebop prose" had seduced me when I was a teenager, but now in Paris I also fell for the prose (the novels, but I soon switched to the essays, which I keep reading & rereading to this day) of James Baldwin. My roommate at Shakespeare & Company — my dad had cut me off financially because of my dropping out — turned out to be a Moroccan writer called Mohammed Khaïr-Eddine. He showed me early Moroccan avant-garde writing, both poetry & prose — the work of the *Souffles* group, primarily, to which he belonged with Abdellatif Laâbi — & turned me on to the Algerian novelist Kateb Yacine's *Nedjma*. Here was a writing that was at boiling point in terms of language, with an intensity that simply did away with those formal genre borders of "poetry" or "prose." This was "writing writing" as Gertrude Stein would have said! Writing by someone who wasn't French but who used French in ways the French had never thought of using it. As Kateb Yacine said when he was asked after Algerian independence was won, whether he was henceforth going to write in Arabic: "No, we won the war. We're keeping French as the spoils of war. And we do with it what we want." In that sense, he invented a new poly-lyrical (yes, "political" sounds along here) language, as Habib Tengour does too. [*Turns to Habib Tengour in the audience.*] That made a difference, compared to the Parisian "ron-ron" of that big laundry basket of novels that come out every fall — actually, the best, if not the cheapest sleeping pills I know of.

You say that you didn't publish this wonderful, I'm sure, novel.

It was terrible!

Yet, when you gave An American Suite *to me, you wrote on the front page "mes erreurs, je veux dire errances de jeunesse." What I got from that, but also from your whole work, is that there are very few things of which you say, "Well, I was young …" It seems that you still cherish the things that you wrote at a younger age. So I was wondering why that novel would be treated that way. Because it's a novel?*

I'll tell you why. One of the poems in the book you mention recalls a concert conducted by Pierre Boulez. My readings of Boulez's writings as well as my experience of his music, & the context of that experience in London's Round House allowed me to create a structure for that poem. It's a playful investigation of how a musical structural thought like Boulez's can, if it can, enter a poem. That aborted novel was about me not getting laid because the girl I thought I had in bed went off with somebody else — that's the most boring possible subject in the world, & the level of my writing wasn't able to move it into some other sphere either.

OK, but wouldn't that fit into a poem?

A bad poem, yes, most of the time! That's what I told my students when I had to teach creative writing. The first thing I told them on opening day — in order to shock them out of any complacency — was: "How many of you are there in this class? 25. In five years, only one of you — at the most! — will still be writing. How can that be? Because you will all get laid, i.e. come into a more or less good & satisfying sex life & have a partner & forget all about writing." This was for undergraduates. There's a basic sense I have, namely that people want to be creative in some, even in many ways, & are, & try writing or painting or acting or singing & there's nothing wrong with that, of course, to the contrary. But in my area, poetry, the universities have instituted a wide gamut of creative writing courses — financial milk-cows for the institutions — which amount to a way of artificially creating "professional poets." After 2 or 4 or 5 years they hand you a creative writing degree that claims that you are now officially a poet. I don't think this works & it is not good for poetry. It's a weird con job, really a classical Ponzi scheme: the universities make money because the students pay, once they have their degree certifying them as poets, & one or maybe 2 books published by small presses or presses dependent in one way or another on the writing programs in the universities, as there is no money in poetry as such anyway, all they can do is look for a job teaching — creative writing! And so the creative writing departments get larger & new ones are set up, & more people become certified poets looking for jobs teaching creative writing …

And most of those courses & departments depend on a poetics that does not interest me, the poetics of the personal narrative where the judgment of how good the poetry is based on how "true" it is to the writer's experience. That inane question of "finding your voice!" I always told my students: "Why don't you get cough syrup if you lost your voice? You have your voice, there's nothing you can do about it. So listen to other people's voices. Translate. Go & find what is happening around you & elsewhere in the world. That's where the poetry is." I basically stopped teaching creative writing & changed those "writing" courses into translation seminars with a theoretical background of comparative literature.

I think we're back to poetry, because we've exhausted the novel subject. When I read the title An American Suite, *it reminds me of Bach's music:* French Suites, English Suites... *Yet, in your poetry, classical or baroque music doesn't come often, it's more contemporary music (you cited Boulez) or jazz; looking at my notes, I can find examples of Stockhausen (*Gesang der Jünglinge*),* Wagner (Tristan *conducted by Furtwängler)... Is there a reason for that, or could it be that I didn't spot references to baroque or classical music? Because the title really makes me think of it.*

Well, a suite can be classical or contemporary. There are rock albums that could be called or that were conceived as "suites." My sense of music is this: I have a rather dead or just bad ear. I cannot play an instrument; I cannot sing ... The tune you all sang earlier [*The session started with the audience singing* Happy Birthday], please don't ask me to sing it. Nicole claims the opposite, that I need to sing, that I should sing, & that I could sing if I only let go.

When I was raised in Ettelbruck — 15 miles from here, & they now call it Ettelbrooklyn, which sounds weirdly funny to me —, the escape was American culture. We were "Pattontown" from the mid-1950s on, because the Rundstedt offensive had come through here & had been pushed back by General Patton's troops, so we had American soldiers coming every year to celebrate this win. On those occasions I would buy second-hand *Playboy* magazines & resell them in high school. I would hear American speech. There was jive talk, southern twangs, Brooklyn intonations — various accents I recognized from the American movies I had seen in grandmother's *Cinéma de la paix*. This was very exciting. I was listening to American AFN radio stations & heard rock 'n' roll & jazz. The very first piece of writing I ever published was a kind of potted biography of

Charlie Parker in the magazine of the *Jeunesse étudiante catholique* — I belonged to this organization for two months before losing my faith. So jazz was core. I often locate the date of my arrival in New York as being "three months after John Coltrane passed." This was very important, because jazz was the essence of music to me, & was certainly essential in my approach to poetry.

Perhaps the one who said this best was an American poet, my old friend Clayton Eshleman, who passed four months ago. He explained that he, as a Midwestern boy who was set down as a kid on the piano to learn how to play, once on the radio heard a song he knew, played by Bud Powell. He listened & said: "Wow! You don't have to imitate exactly what the score in the songbook demands. You can play with that; you can make it up as you go along. You can take off from those indications, vary the song, invent, improvise!" That opened up Eshleman to poetry, to invention, to creativity.

I don't think my interest in jazz came out of an absolute occasion like Clayton's, but there was that same thrill to it. Then in Paris, when I was still in medical school, the little jukebox at the *Petit Bar* on the Place du Petit-Pont — we used to hang out there a lot, but it no longer exists — was playing Bob Dylan, I remember to this day that "D9" was "Rainy Day Women #12 & 35." And two blocks across & up the road was *Aux Trois Mailletz*, where Memphis Slim would play, & we would go there. And in the Rue de la Huchette were *Le Caveau de la Huchette*, *Le Chat qui pêche*, where traditional & avant-garde jazz was available. To me, this was an incredible opening up. I only came back to classical music later, because when we were driven in high school from Diekirch to Luxembourg City to the *Jeunesses musicales* concerts, the third time you heard the same symphony you dashed out as quickly as you could to visit the bookstore nearby & hang out at the just-opened new American-style place for teenagers, Walter's Milk-Bar.

So when I got to America, in 1967, this was a great moment: jazz was very much alive, rock 'n' roll was very much alive. In 1969,

I was on a boat back to Europe after graduating with my parents when Woodstock happened, so I missed it. But I returned three months later to New York, & moved into an apartment one & a half blocks away from the Fillmore East. I could go to concerts there — for free as I had a job as editor of the underground magazine *Corpus*, & thus a press card. This also enabled me to interview Jerry Garcia of the *Grateful Dead*, Ed Sanders of *The Fugs*, & others. So rock 'n' roll was there for those years. But it quickly had to deal with the deaths of the big ones, Hendrix, Joplin, & the one who styled himself as a Rimbaudian poet, Jim Morrison of *The Doors*. Somehow I lost interest in much of rock 'n' roll, but got back into jazz — & have remained there to this day. When I moved to London in 1972 one of my close friends & teachers there was a man called Eric Mottram. My other close friend Allen Fisher & I would be invited every Thursday evening by Eric to his house. He had the best collection of 20th-century classical music. So we would eat together & then spend two hours listening, over a couple of years, to the whole of contemporary music. My education in that area came from Eric. It is also around that time that I saw Pierre Boulez conduct *Parsifal* at the London Opera.

2nd Conversation

September 3, 2021

The beauty of a series of interviews like this one is that we get time to revise previous conversations & I get to think of follow-up questions I didn't think about in the heat of things. Here's one. You mentioned that the novel is a 19th-century genre, mostly with invented characters; you also mentioned that both of your sons are in movies, & from what I know, you actually do like movies. Is it because you grew up watching them in your grandmother's cinema, or do you find something particularly interesting in movies as a 21st-century genre? Because they do mostly have invented characters as well.

I could say that the novel is dead because there is cinema. However, for me, a big problem with cinema in its fixed Hollywoodian genre was to take 300-page novels & adapt them into 90- or 120-minute films in the old days. In that sense, the form that saves what a novel narrative can be is television. You can take any, even a very large, book — let's say Tolstoy's *War and Peace* — & make an even 3-hour movie out of it: you may like the actors, the action or the landscapes, it's still not Tolstoy's book. But if you take, say, Alfred Döblin's *Berlin Alexanderplatz* & have Rainer Werner Fassbinder make a 15-hour TV series out of it, you can get its depth, its richness, different perspectives, & the camera can be very different from the all-knowing *Deus ex typewriter* that the narrator of a novel is. So television helps; there are displacements possible that the 19th-century novel point of view doesn't give you. I think film & television are now extremely interesting for their possible narrative developments. Now, I'm not involved in film myself, or only very liminally via Nicole Peyrafitte who is a filmmaker & video-artist, besides being a painter & performer. But our sons are. Joseph Mastantuono is in Venice right now, because on September 7th & 8th the feature he produced, *Mon père, le diable* — directed by Cameroon-American Ellie Foumbi —, has its premiere.

During the festival?

Actually, their script was chosen & financed by the festival as part of the Biennale Film College. So it's not in competition as such. And my son Miles just made a sequence of six half-hour or 35 minutes films that are going to be picked up by a television network for streaming. He wrote the script of what is genre-wise a thriller-drama & filmed it as a series: it's a very different sense in the creation, blocking, & so on, than it would be if you'd condense a novel into a 90-minute film. I think seeing people in films, actors & actresses — but also on stage, as I love theater —, enacting characters & bringing them to life is something totally different from reading a novel & extracting the character from print. So yes, film is relevant. Inescapable, in fact, for my generation of writers. Even at the level of the family: it was my father's father who built the first movie-house in Ettelbruck, the *Cinéma de la paix*, facing the church — I have written in detail about this elsewhere, so won't repeat it all here — but certainly my enduring love for traditional genre films, detective thriller but before all westerns came as much from the films I saw as a kid than from the Karl May novels. But I would learn a lot after leaving Ettelbruck — first in Luxembourg City, then in Paris, & later in New York — from more avant-garde, experimental films, made from the 1950s to the 1980s in America, but also other places, like Europe, France for example — but the French always think they're *the* avant-garde! — but also majorly from Germany's new cinema. My friend Ody Roos & I were together in Paris as students, him at the Institut des hautes études cinématographiques & me in medical school: he stayed on to become a filmmaker in France & I went on to become a poet in the United States. He once said to me: "When you left for America, I should probably have gone to Germany." Because this was where a new cinema was coming from, rather than this self-commenting, reflective French Nouvelle Vague or post-Nouvelle Vague. (The best representative of which actually became a Swiss citizen — Godard!) For me two German filmmakers of my own generation have remained central: Wenders & Fassbinder.

I didn't know much about American avant-garde cinema at that time because it wasn't available in Europe, at least not to me. But after I came to the US in 1967 I discovered it, or rather I was told by poets to check it out, as there was a strong connection between experimental poets & filmmakers. Stan Brakhage, for example, was someone who was also very much influenced by the poets & influenced poets in return: he thus made a sequence of 8-mm films called *Songs* — which title, he told Robert Kelly, he'd gotten from Kelly, so Kelly, in turn, wrote a book of 30 poems called *Songs*, dedicated to Brakhage. Both men also had a huge correspondence (that needs publishing!). In the 1960s, the artist — & writer — Carolee Schneemann made groundbreaking avant-garde movies, such as *Viet-Flakes*, a major statement against the Vietnam War. She also practiced a very personal erotic cinema, taking a camera to bed with her & her husband to make *Fuses* in 1967.

Those films or film sequences, in their thinking about film & their consciousness about the nature of their material base, were very close to how the poets were thinking about their material, that is, the nature of language & how to work with this language material as *prima materia*. Stan Brakhage wrote a small book called *A Moving Picture Giving and Taking Book*, in which he tells you that if you want to make movies, what you do is to get into a dark room, open a can of film, & then start drawing & imprinting directly on film, frame after frame, & experiment with how light imprints on it. You use the material itself, the *pellicule*, like you paint on canvas or carve wood: you draw or scratch it, then you can layer/collage elements, single frames or longer strips one on top of the other, etc. At that level, cinema was always present & very interesting to me. Later on I got to know Jonas Mekas & the New York Film Archive, but it was Brakhage, Schneemann, & those artists that I liked & learned the most from at that time. They were essential for me as a developing poet.

But you've never ventured into script writing for the cinema?

Oh, I have done some scripts!

And you do have some ready?

No, but I actually have some script ideas I would like to develop if I get around to it. Obviously, having sons in the trade, I figured maybe they would pick them up! I am kidding... I did write scripts professionally at one point, though: I was briefly a freelance rewriting department. In 1985, 1986, & early 1987, a number of American filmmaking companies set up shop in Europe because it was cheaper to film in Bulgaria, Czechoslovakia, or Spain than in America. So their offices in Paris had a problem: they had scripts that were supposed to be shot in Texas & now needed to be shot in Bulgaria. I can't remember how it came about, somebody must have told me, who was living in Paris at the time, & I figured I could do that — especially as they paid pretty well, of course. Now, you only had 48 hours or so to reorient the script that had been set in Mendocino County, California, to now be set on the Black Sea coast. And you had to take one or two characters out because they didn't have that actress... So I rewrote half a dozen scripts in 48-hour periods, & that was good money. I have no idea what ever happened to them. It was what the French in a rather racist manner call "travail de nègre."

One reason that work interested me — beyond paying the rent — was that I had done an oral autobiography of Samuel Fuller, the American director, for France Culture, & one evening when Sam & I were having dinner, he explained to me that I should be involved in film because, as he laid it out, "the most important person is the writer — actors & directors are a dime a dozen & interchangeable, what makes a good movie is a well-written story."

Pour la petite histoire, my "career" in film started when I was ten or eleven in Luxembourg, when my father had a patient — I have forgotten his name — who was with Télé Luxembourg. They wanted to do a little adventure movie for kids, some kind of imitation *Rin-Tin-Tin*. I had a friend in the Ardennes who had this big German shepherd we would play & run in the forest with, & my father must have told his patient. So Télé Luxembourg comes & sets up a little story where something (or someone?) gets lost, & my friend & I & the dog are filmed working in the forest & that film was shown on Luxembourg television. I don't think I ever saw it, I just remember doing the film. That was also the end of my career in cinema in Luxembourg. At one point in Paris I made 100 dollars or so for being an extra in a scene of, I think it was, *What's New, Pussycat?* that was cut later as I never saw it when I watched the film. I am also an extra in the film *Mon père, le diable* I mentioned earlier, that is shown in Venice & that Joseph is the producer of, with my mother in law, & I actually have one line & she does too. Nicole has done a number of videos of me — interviews, readings, etc. But that's all …

I'm looking forward to seeing you in your latest role!

Now, seriously, I have a couple of scripts in mind, but I have never gotten around to finalize them — or even expand them beyond the stage of an abstract. They were initially conceived as plays for theater. *The Agony of I.B.*, my play about Ingeborg Bachmann & Paul Celan, was first imagined as a film. That would however be a complex & more experimental film, as most of the action is set during the heroine's final coma, where she is visited by the important men in her life, in fact & finally, only in her imagination. It's a realm of in-between-ness, an imaginary realm that interests me a lot, as you can tell from the title of one of my poetry collections — *Barzakh*, the Arabic name for the realm between life & death, what the Tibetans call the Bardo. Happily the offer came to do a play for the Théâtre National in Luxembourg, & I think it worked out better as a stage play. However a film version is still something on my mind. There is another film that I wanted to do; the problem is that I have to find a woman figure for it, because it's all men in the 15th century. It is set in Damascus under attack by the Mongols, led by Timur or Tamburlaine, who is also the main character of the theater play *Tamburlaine the Great* by Christopher Marlowe. A beautiful thing happened during the siege: the great Ibn Khaldun, a Maghrebi & the first sociologist & a major historian had been called by the caliph in Cairo & made a judge there. When the Damascus caliph came under attack, they went to Damascus to assist their friend. Timur knew that Ibn Khaldun was in town, & wanted to meet him. Obviously the caliph didn't like the idea of Ibn Khaldun associating with the Mongol enemy. So Khaldun was let down over the rampart-wall in the middle of the night, in a basket, & went over to the khan's tent. They talked for two days about the world, about everything. And then Ibn Khaldun got back in, after having been promised by Timur that poets & writers would be spared. That to me was a fascinating subject & I've thought of it for twenty years now; but I somehow never got down to write it. Maybe my telling it is my writing of it & maybe this interview will be the completion of that idea, who knows?

I remember that we talked once about this idea when we discussed The Agony of I.B., *because it was the other possibility you had to develop into a play.*

That's right. I also talked about it with Miles the other day, because I came home & suddenly had the insight: yes, I know how to do it. It's going to be the 1,002nd Arabian Tale, a new Scheherazade, a contemporary Arab woman in the context of contemporary Syria telling the tale of that time. So I would get a woman as a core voice in it.

This sounds like a good plot! Now we've talked a lot about movies, a bit about theater. I wanted to ask you, in order to somehow close this "genre review," about opera. I do remember — I think it was in 2016 — you mentioning that you had a project of an opera libretto. Is it still in the making?

Nothing is in the making, but there were two projects, which could possibly be reanimated, if the occasion presents itself. After I did *The Gulf (Between You & Me)* — commissioned by Donald Nally for his superb ensemble, *The Crossing*, — a musical piece with three composers, one of these, Gene Coleman, asked me if I would be interested to work on an opera about the life of Buckminster Fuller. I thought it a fascinating idea, because I am really a fan of Fuller's. He was one the 20th-century visionaries, also attached to poetry in odd ways: he was connected to Black Mountain College & wrote in what he called not poetry but "ventilated prose." That's a great line! Fuller was one of the great crazy inventors & thinkers of the 20th century in America. You have to realize that thinking is not just philosophy or theory, there's thinking also in industry, technology, architecture — in fact in all aspects of human endeavor. The geodesic dome & the housing that Fuller invented are amazing. Now we had not worked out yet how this would look in an opera, & it kind of got put on the back-burner: Gene got involved in other projects, & I did too in order to finish my Celan translation work, especially the amazing posthumous prose gatherings of *Microliths They Are, Little Stones*, for his 100th birth year in 2020.

    I came up with another idea during that time: one of my favorite poets as a young man was Matsuo Bashō — he came back recently in my poetry when I wrote *The Book of U*, a sequence of poems that all feature cormorants. I bought a first book by Bashō in 1965 at the *Gagliani* bookstore in Paris, & I still have it here. The second book by him I bought was in America, when Clayton Eshleman pointed out to me that Cid Corman had just brought out a translation of Bashō's great travel diary, *Back Roads to Far Towns* (*Oku no hosomichi*). I was thinking about that book at the moment of the Fukushima disaster, because Bashō's road led past that town. This idea came to me for an opera where four non-Japanese (European, American, African) people decide to go on a pilgrimage in homage to Bashō, walking the same road — from Tokyo up north, then west across the country & down to Kyoto. Gene, who spent time in Japan & often uses Japanese instruments, was very interested. So I applied for a grant to go to Japan for six months to write this. I didn't get it at first, & when it was time to apply again, a certain thing called Covid-19 happened...

Did you make it to Japan in the end?

No. Japan is a country I have never been in, but that is important to me in terms of poetry. I am always associated with America, right? Well, it could have turned out different: in December 1967 I drove with my poet friend & co-student at Bard, Stephen Kessler — someone who wrote great baseball poems, way back then, which was a surprising area for me as a would-be Euro-intellectual! — from Bard College in upstate New York to Los Angeles in his Porsche. That was my first time on the road in America, & of course I was ecstatic for the whole trip ... until we rolled the car three times on a snowed- & iced-over Route 66 in Arizona & had to huddle in a police car trying to get warm! But I didn't just want to go to L.A.: the reason I traveled was that my friend David Eyre, whom I met in Paris in 1965, was getting married to his Swedish girlfriend Eva whom he had met in Paris too. He was a high school teacher in

Honolulu, Hawaii. I had promised to be his best man. So from L.A. I flew to Hawaii. He set me up on Diamond Head, this beautiful area of Honolulu, with his parents who had this little Japanese gardener's house in back of their property. This became my house. I had of course brought one of the Blyth volumes, & so while I was sitting there — maybe for the first time cross-legged on floor mats — I started wondering: "Shall I go on? I could be in Kyoto in a few days, & meet up with Gary Snyder & Cid Corman, get more into Zen — which was interesting me at the time —, get more into Japanese language & poetry?"

The reason haiku had interested me was that my English was still a Luxemburger's English: very short poems that are very tight with words were a way of hiding a lack of knowledge while learning about how things worked in this new language. If I ever publish a *Collected Poems*, the opening section will in all likelihood consist of the four or six haiku I kept from that period. I mean, they're not very Japanese haiku. Let me tell you the first one, which I actually know by heart: "Autumn leaves / on clear rocks / in a double Scotch."

So, back on Oahu, in January 1968, I was really wondering whether I should return to Bard College. I had a job as a waiter & sommelier in the Oahu Hilton — there are great stories attached to it that I'll have to write down at some point —, so I was making a bit of money. I didn't like the Hawaiian society very much; it was a very strange place, kind of a racial *mille-feuille*, a rather rigid & visible class or better color-coded caste structure. And I really thought hard during those weeks about moving on to Kyoto but I caught myself: "Yes, but you want to write in English, so you should go back, because you are not yet done with America." I flew back to San Francisco, where I stayed a few days; those were crazy acid days, I don't remember anything except a lot of colors. Then I flew back to New York & Bard College to finish my first year there. So there was this whole idea of pushing toward the East. Gary Snyder, in that sense, as a poet, was very, very important for me among the so-called Beats. I guess I had already read Jack Kerouac's book where Snyder is the central character, *The Dharma Bums*. There was a strong attraction, which has remained, even if on the back burner.

We started to speak about cinema, & I remember that at Bard at that time Kurosawa movies were beginning to be shown. There was this interesting notion of contemporary art & film in Japan. Kurosawa was very important also because there was a remake of his samurai movie, *Seven Samurai (Shichinin no samurai)*, as an American movie called *The Magnificent Seven*, with Yul Brynner, Steve McQueen, Horst Buchholz … I remember seeing both of them & wondering whether the American movie was just an imitation, just using the samurai genre to make another oater as we say, a western, or whether there was something else coming in there. I love both movies, & I don't mind if one rips off the other to some extent for its plot. The samurai movie has a strangeness that it never lost, whereas westerns became much more familiar, even way too obvious in their oversimplified mythologizing of America, even when, as in this one, the American heroes go into Mexico. On that first road trip, my first venture into the actual "Wild West," when we rolled the car, the cops drove us to, & we ended up spending Christmas afternoon in, a bus stop in what is in fact an actual ghost-town, called Two Guns, Arizona, deserted except for four cowboys playing poker at the next table. We, with our slightly long hair, & somewhat hippy-ish in our dress too, were sitting there kind of freaked out until the Greyhound bus came & we could ride the dog to Tinsel Town!

Well, I planned for this conversation to start talking about movies & then get back to music in poetry, where we stopped last time. But we already spent almost all of our time on the follow-up questions … which means that it was a good idea to bring up the subject! So instead of getting back to music, I'd like to ask a last question for today. We talked movies, we talked theater, we talked opera: I understand that, for you, genres are not fixed & can be intertwined, but is there one that we haven't touched upon & that you also find relevant for the 21st century?

I think that the 21st century will have to invent its own genre, & it will come into being without anybody knowing what it is, what it will be, beforehand. Everybody will be thinking that they're doing something new but all of a sudden someone will turn around & point at some specific thing & exclaim: "Ah! That's a 21st-century work." I'm imagining, early in the 20th century, Gertrude Stein sitting down & beginning to write her portraits & somehow realizing she had to change the prose away from Flaubert's. And so in the process of trying to get to what she saw happening around her, the portraits evolved into Gertrude Stein's prose genre. This is however a process. As primarily a poet, I may be accused by some of a certain arrogance & entitlement, as I like to claim that the genre of poetry is the most capacious one into which you can put everything. What the 20th century did magnificently with poetry was to explode it qua genre so that you can not only have a Baudelairian prose poem in it, but you have "actual" prose in a poem. You can play with that. Why not have drawings in a poem? Why not have bits of dialogue? A musical score? Why not have philosophy? Or scientific discourse? In that sense, the long poem to me seems to be the great advance in the second part of the 20th century. Away from the notion of the epic — I already mentioned that in our first conversation. When you get through Pound ("through" in both senses of that word) to Charles Olson, when you get to Louis Zukofsky, the long poem, or the serial poem, whatever you want to call it, as an American genre is really a tremendous advance. My sense is that this may be expanded even more, into what Robert Duncan called the "grand collage" — also mentioned earlier —, that is the imaginative formal structure with which I, as a 20th-century person but riding the two centuries, can try to make sense of what I should be doing for the years I got left. We have major examples of such works, from the great long works by Rachel Blau DuPlessis or Alice Notley to those of Nathaniel Mackey or Will Alexander. And younger poets & artists will find their own ways to expand on these matters so as to get into poetry what they need to make or at least help to make their, our world, cohere.

Thank you very much, Pierre. We'll call it a day for today, & next time we will definitely go back to music in poetry.

3rd Conversation

October 4, 2021

As promised in our initial conversation, I'd like to continue on music in poetry. The first question is building upon the poem you wrote about Pierre Boulez conducting. In this piece, you use a variety of visual effects on the page: different lengths of tabulation, blank lines, spaces within words, underlining, capital letters, even a hand-written curved line. This variety of effects can be found throughout your poetry. Would it be right to compare them to instructions on a musical score?

You can think along such lines, indeed. They are not, however, meant to be that directly. There is of course a whole wing of poetry called visual & sound poetry, & my work doesn't really fall into those categories directly, but plays with, borrows, some elements from their formal procedures. There are of course innumerable different ways of disposing words on the page, & yes, in the case of the poem you mention, it does include such notational aspects that should indicate to the reader that the poem wants to be read aloud, that that is one of its modes.

 I heard a wonderful example of such a poem two nights ago, when Charles Bernstein read at the Morgan Library here in New York. One of the poems in *topsy-turvy*, his new book, called "A Poet Supreme" is dedicated to the great jazz pianist & poet Cecil Taylor. Charles had the poem printed with different letters & words having different colors, creating a kind of color code. Here's a picture of it:

A POET SUPREME

I'vE gOt sPaSmodIc rhYthM yOu'Ve got **il-li-li-lo-(o!)-*q*-shuN** As seNsOry mode/or release, g(-el-eL-)ation, revER-(b)urr-er-er-atIon, recoMbinatiOn, oVerlAy, impppUlse, proPulSe, dash-0'-tHe-puddinGed-puddLe-minded *breath turn* AS woE-inGLy wiGkles, waitiNg, whOa-wh-w-hImsey, jeRkeD as celeStial harmoniCs/harmonicKs, so sL(0!)W yOu can heAr the vibRatIons lasHing agaInSt tHe dOrmeRs. <<¶§∞¢£¶>> *ich habe einen spontanen Rhythmus, du hast il-li-li-lo- (o!) - q-sun als sensor-modus / oder freigabe, g (-el-el-) aktion, ÜberLieB, Atmen drehen sich wie wEi-ingly: dOrMeRen hören können.* ⟨§∿⇒→∞>⇐ʒ↑⇑∿≰⩙⇐. IncLudiNg but not limItEd t0. ⇐ʒ∞>↑ dreamT (screamT) beComEs wHiPlaSh/wishlist w-w-wiTHerEd wHisPs, SprUnG suCcessiOn oVertoWeD to dArn-daRe-upSter FLOURESCENT **eMManaShUNs**, sHoWereD by bL0o(uh)ms, beGaLeD, likk*k*e a GahZheal doink bAcK fl00ps on a corn foLD. //√¶§∞•≠\\ *incluindo, mas não limitado >> sonhou (grita) benewlal / w-w-werered, pesquisado por bloo (uh) bem-vindo, talvez um em um fiorde de dobra.* ⟨§∿⇒→ʒ↑>⇐⇑∿≰⩙∞⇐. What a FluKe! iF I cOulD onLy sing 0ut o' temmpi-MENTAL. **CrEaTiOnIsMus(e)** begins *here*. mInEd-f0rGed in surrep(E)titious eruptions (scrum-uhm-p-p-p-tious), mired |) smeared (| in *tenebrae*—aCcouStic tAcTil(t)itY nigh onto sTeAm pour-r-r-r-ing (purrrrring) oUt of man(w)Hole. → ʒ↑>⇐⇑⟨⇒§∿∿≰⩙∞⇐ Qu'est-ce qu'un FluKe! Si je ne faisais que chanter |]} commence ici dans éruptions mérieuses, embourbés |) enduit (| dans le tenebrae - tactilité acoustique [inclinaison] près de la vapeur qui sort de la bouche d'égout. INCLUS, mais pas limité à. **caL-Q!-luSt** *of* inter-per-s0nic quest-IONs. thE makiNg iS the RE:seiv̵eing, roiLinG with *& again*St— aLl tH(w)aætttt re-v(h)eAls in rE-veiIiNg.

for Cecil Taylor

When he reads it, it becomes very much a sound poem. He pronounces every single letter & word as printed — so the visual score becomes/is a score for sound reading. It was the first time in years I heard such a poem read as well as Kurt Schwitters read his. For people like Jerome Rothenberg & myself, who published a large English edition of his writings some years ago, Schwitters, who was doing this kind of work from the 1920s to the 1950s, is a kind of absolute poet in that specific way of working with language. For 20th-century literature, Schwitters's *Ursonate* is, at least for us, as important as Joyce's *Finnegans Wake*. When you read the *Wake*, a lot of it is sound play. It's not written like a score, it's an ongoing prose affair, but if you try to read the *Wake* aloud, you are continuously caught up in sound play. You move in different languages, you move along vectors of *polyvalence*. So I think that prose, poetry, & music (painting too, all the arts in fact) entered the 20th century with permissions & examples by 19th-century forerunners (see our opening chapter in *Poems for the Millennium* vol. 1, called "Forerunners") & invented the forms the 20th century needed: multiple, open-ended possibilities & procedures. If we take for example musical composition, the old staff notation of traditional European "classical" music turns out to be too limiting for what many if not most contemporary composers want — actually, need — to use in terms of sound, pitch, duration, etc. Their notes fall off those five-line staves & tumble all over the place — a little bit like a cartoon where someone's voice or instrument would shake the staves & the notes can't hang on & fall or fly off like birds from telephone wires. So new notational systems have to be invented, at least for those compositions — music- or language-based — that need to be preserved for future reading or performance, i.e. that are not part of that other contemporary art mode, namely improvisation.

A book that was also important to me — & to a lot of poets, I think — was John Cage's 1969 *Notations*, an anthology of contemporary musical scores. With developments & technical innovations in the 20th century, composers had new instruments available — electronic instruments, for example, plus studio techniques & so on — & had to invent a new way of representing, of scoring their music on the notational page, because that's what you need to do in order for other musicians to be able to perform your compositions. That anthology, *Notations*, was amazing: what I, as a poet, could learn from it was the fact that depending on what sounds/meanings/effects you want to produce, you have to invent a new way of writing these down. In the most basic sense, you could say that a poem, true to what the 20th century opened up, couldn't really fit anymore into the old notation-modes of, for example, the sonnet/sonata or some such fixed formal structure. Again, it's the already mentioned sentence that was so important to me as a 15-year-old, Rimbaud saying about Baudelaire: "You can't put new wine into old bottles."

Now what's really important too, when talking about music & poetry, is that at that time you had a range of musical possibilities. You had people like Boulez, an extremely controlled man in his musical composition (& conducting), & on the other hand you had Cage, who was completely open, manipulating instruments, including chance occurrences (outside sound coming in from an open window, say) & so on. For me, what was even more central — & this has remained in a way so to this day, even if, as I am editing this part of our interview, I am listening to Alicia de Larrocha playing Robert Schuman's *Piano Concerto in A Minor, Opus 54* —, was jazz & how it moved from its more traditional forms coming out of the blues, into & through big orchestral forms, & then into be-bop, which was of course the revolution of that moment of the late 1940s early 1950s, for the generation that preceded mine. Listening to Coltrane, even today, makes me think: "Wow! This is where new things, where new ideas are continuously happening." You're not playing a melody that is pretty because it's repeated & you love & can rest & relax — thus feel safe & secure — in this repetition, but you're taking five notes you may know from a popular song &

you begin to play with them, loosen them from their old structure, heighten them, lower them, turn them around, look at them from different angles, etc.

How do you translate this into poem-writing?

That's actually how I like to write. What happens is that I may see an advertisement on a billboard, hear in the street below my window someone say something for which I have no context, read by chance across two independent columns in a newspaper, whatever, & that can get me going. This is of course a totally common experience & everybody has at some point in their life played with & done collages. A lovely example of integrating such an event into a poem is Paul Blackburn's wonderful poem where he's sitting in his favorite coffee shop, writing, as a typical American troubadour of the late 1950s or early 1960s. So while writing, he looks up for no apparent reason & there's this truck in front of the café with one of its back doors open; on the one visible door, he reads the three letters: "zen." This is great, he thinks, & then the truck driver comes & closes the door, & now Paul can read three more letters — "fro" —, combining of course into the word "frozen." That little word cut-up now enters the poem underhand & creates a space there from which the poet — & the reader — can "riff," to use a musical term, & move on.

 I was extremely impressed early on by the connection between live voice & poetry in America; we didn't have that much anymore in Europe, where poetry was essentially printed matter to be read in the silent privacy of your study or living room or bed, whatever. It was the Beats who revived public readings, the famous example being the Six Gallery reading in San Francisco in 1955, also with the connection to jazz that came in afterwards. I love reading with jazz musicians, with improvised music. Among my own favorite readings I gave over the years were those in the 1980s with Steve

Lacy, the great soprano saxophonist — we got to work together a few times in Paris & Rotterdam. I like it when the musicians don't actually read ("study") the poems beforehand, when they experience them "live," in situ, & something happens … or doesn't, but that's the risk that makes the adventure thrilling.

So music to me has been core in those multiple senses. Now I mentioned in our first conversation that I am tone-deaf. When I turned 50, some 25 years ago, I foolishly — & only half jokingly — said: "OK, I'm quitting poetry & from now on I'll try to become John Coltrane." So Nicole offered me an alto saxophone as a birthday present & I began playing, thinking: "Maybe I can get something going." I couldn't. I played for a couple of months, made some, rather futile sounds, then put the instrument back in its box … it is still there though, not 6 feet from where I am sitting, hiding behind a row of folders containing a range of my writings … I can't really play music & it's a great regret. I found a photo the other day taken on the back terrace of my parents' house in Ettelbruck, in which I, 14 or 15, am dressed in a sort of improvised Hawaiian gear & hold & seem to strum a guitar, so my interest or desire dates back a long time. It's also a generational thing: in my generation, you may have wanted to become a poet, but the most popular generational mode was rock 'n' roll. Jim Morrison of *The Doors* always said: "I'm a poet first & second only a rock singer." There was this generational sense that the rock song could be the right form for poetry. There were great examples like the more political folk music or Bob Dylan. In that sense, I was not surprised when they gave the Nobel Prize to Dylan: his *œuvre* is as much his written words as songs than the notes he clothed them in. It's a *Gesamtkunstwerk*. We all thought: "Well, maybe that's the way to go." At Bard College, when I was an undergraduate, three doors down the hall was Donald Fagen's room; Walter Becker was in another dorm & the two formed Steely Dan a couple of years later. If you listen to this band's lyrics, you have a sense that literature comes in.

The name of the band itself comes from Burroughs's *Naked Lunch*, a book I had carried with me from Luxembourg to Bard & lent to everyone who wanted to read it. It was my bible at that time (still is, to my mind, one of, if not the most accurate political analysis of the century — of this one too, so far).

So I see a lot of connections between popular music, "serious" classical music, jazz ... even though these groupings do not come together or meet very often. But if you lived in New York, you could catch Ornette Coleman one night & Janis Joplin the next & get into a bar fight with Leonard Cohen at the El Quijote bar in the Chelsea Hotel ... as I did! Is that what you were asking me about music?

Well, what I find fascinating is that whatever the question is, you always manage to say something interesting on the subject, which makes my job very easy. Even though my initial question was a technical one, yes, you've already covered a lot on the subject of music & poetry, & beautifully. There's one thing you talked about that strikes me, related to the music of words. I noted something important you said in an interview: "Although my work was never theatrical [that was at a time you hadn't written The Agony of I.B.*], it has always been tied to public performance. Public readings are an essential component of American poetry — so in a way my poems are similar to music scores that need to be interpreted on stage to be complete." So are there any "tricks" that you use to give readers the experience of a read poem, even though it is only written? How is the experience not totally lost on a printed page?*

I think the layout on the page in that sense can be seen & used as a musical notation: the rhythm of the lines, the length of the lines, the *enjambments*, how words are broken up — I do that a lot —, the spacing ... That is, when you read a poem — a contemporary poem, not just one of mine —, you have to read the pages, which means you also read the white spaces. In a way, that goes all the way back to Mallarmé. One could even make a case & suggest that a more traditional form such as the sonnet (even the name has a musical assonance) was a way of transcribing a musical idea, no?

Indeed, Jennifer Moxley mentions the Coup de dés *by Mallarmé in her essay about your work called "Dérive-ations," which is part of Peter Cockelbergh's* Pierre Joris: Cartographies of the In-Between.

Yes, so the poem is a score. Now, every interpretation, as you know from classical music, is different. When you hear Glenn Gould playing Bach on the piano, that's totally different from what, say Alicia de Larrocha (who right now, as I am here in the editing of this part of the interview, is playing Bach!) did. I always loved hearing those differences. In London, in the 1970s, when I heard Boulez conduct Wagner's *Parsifal*, I could not think of two more different musical possibilities. Most people dismissed Boulez as a composer & said he was only a great conductor, but I always thought he was a totally great composer too. So to see him conduct something that at one level seems to be totally opposite to his own music was stunning. I loved his *Parsifal*; it's my favorite interpretation, because something *happens*. When Boulez reads the score in his very specific, clear-sighted way, Wagner, who can easily get muggy, benefits from this.

 That being said, I can only add that I am a total amateur when it comes to any kind of music. Nicole is of course a much more musically-savvy person & she has put some of my poems to music. To be able to actually create music is amazing to me … *ça m'ébahit!* Her sense of music — or generally of the arts — makes her at home in drawing or visual arts as well as in sound or music. Yesterday, when we were kayaking on the Hudson River, she began singing a song she wrote called *Mahicanituck*,[6] which is Manhattan's original

6. Listen to it here:
 https://music.apple.com/us/album/mahicanituck/218185051?i=218185209

Native American name, naming "a river that flows both ways." It was wonderful being on the Hudson with Nicole singing this poem written as a song. I'm kind of jealous of her ability to do that because, as you know, I can't even sing *Happy Birthday* without many false notes.

But you do have a sincere, heartfelt sensibility to music that not everybody has, so I guess it compensates somehow. You mentioned earlier that word-cuts happen quite often in your poetry. I noted one example I like very much in Barzakh (p. 75), a poem about 9/11. It goes: "this moment / this second / cuts in be- // tween the two."

The intent of the cut is here rather obvious; we know exactly what you mean. But visual effects are not always this transparent to the reader. Is there a conscious visual grammar for your poetry? Are there things that you use consistently to obtain certain effects?

Yes, sometimes, I do this because I want a very specific meaning to appear. Sometimes, I also want to leave all the possibilities of meaning such a cut creates open for the reader to play with. The "cuts in be- // tween the two" is at the most obvious level a visual pun, but the "be" of "between" is also the verb to be, i.e. being is to be in-between. All those things come in here. And then it goes on: "It will be the — [I interrupt myself] / where to breathe / the [I'm going back supposedly to that previous 'the'] or a o- / pen pore." All of a sudden it turns nearly or briefly into an actual sound poem here. Breath comes in, the importance of breathing for life. And obviously you hear "o," "a," "o," then "e," "o," "e," until that becomes the "riots of air." So, yes, it's a whole little musical construction. I don't necessarily notate with one very specific aim in mind. To go back to a reason I don't much like novels, I don't like to know from the beginning what happens at the end (of course there are some novels where that isn't so). The whole pleasure of writing a poem, at least for me, is that you don't have a clue about what's going to happen in the next line, where the poem is going. If I knew, I wouldn't need to write it. I'm writing myself toward something; it's a discovery. Sometimes this discovery can go via a couple of vowels that all of a sudden appear, stand out, in an odd, strange — *ostranenie* — way. And this poem we're talking about goes on playing: it's a "rift in time" that "marks time," so you have a split in time that is also a mark of time. Here you are: you have a musical score. Note that I give the date & also the exact time at the end, 7:20 AM. I'm talking here about a definite mark in time: a "rift in time" that "marks time," a "gash / curled high in air." An hour later, my friend Don Byrd calls me & says: "Please turn your television on." The first plane had flown into the World Trade Center. Somehow there was something that the poem knew that morning & that I didn't know. That's why I put the date on it. I often date a poem, or rather the notebook page, before writing it, like a journal entry; here, the title is "9/11/01" & if I published it like that, one might think: "Oh, he's writing about something that happened." I wrote it two hours before what happened that day, so I thought it was important to add the time at the end — which nearly becomes an integral part of the poem itself rather than an added notation.

I used this poem to ask about word cuts, but you've provided great insight into the whole piece, still linking it to our theme of the day, music in poetry. We talked a lot about sound, but not so much about rhythm. What occurred to me in rereading your works is that one of its characteristics is the use of parentheses. They contain things that you add, information about geography, quotes, things that what you just wrote reminds you of... It kind of interrupts the flow of the poem, creating a very particular rhythm. Do you rework your poems to create this or do you just capture your flow of thoughts?

Both, but it mainly comes in the flow. The poem always has connections to the outside world — the birds, the trees, the cars in the street, the ads on the trucks … — & to my personal world, as well as to what surrounds me here in my study, where I mostly write, thus to all the accumulated books. A poem is always talking to other poets & other poems. Very often, references like you mention come in & I open a parenthesis to give the information. It seems to me very important that the poet be clear about where she gets her information from, in order to lay all the cards out on the table. I could just quote Blackburn, without mentioning him, which would be an arrogant suggestion to the literary *cognoscenti* that Joris knows his stuff, knows of what he talks & maybe a less knowledgeable reader will do the work & try to locate the origins of the quote. But no, I prefer to put Blackburn's name into an open parenthesis — I often don't close it, because then the word leads back directly into the poem. Then the reader who doesn't know PB can ask herself: "Who's that?" & go out & locate that information. I don't want to give the image that I know & that the poem knows, but that the reader should have to decode it somehow. The poem isn't a secret treasure trove you have to dig up & decode. Open field is a concept we discussed earlier on, so everything can come in, the information & where you get it from can also — must — come into the poem right away. It's like forcing the food makers to put on the box exactly what goes into their product. You don't want to sell buyers crap. Is that really chicken in those chicken nuggets or it is recomposed pseudo-meat? I think it's a necessary part of an artist's honesty.

Doesn't this transparency through parentheses, though, mean that you're not in control anymore of the overall rhythm of the poem?

No. Actually, it enriches the possible rhythms of the poem. I don't have a rhythm in mind when I start. Whatever reason the poem has, it starts with a certain way of moving, then interrupts itself for a moment & goes on back to that or creates a new rhythm, maybe a complex combination of those two previous possibly contradictory events. It feels like I'm blowing on my saxophone & suddenly the drummer comes in with a certain beat & I figure out that we can move on that way. If we want to go back to the musical metaphors we've been using throughout today's conversation, the poem becomes a multi-instrumental move with polyrhythms.

4th Conversation

October 18, 2021

In our previous discussion, you talked about "an artist's honesty," which is to transparently give all necessary references to the reader — to "lay all the cards out on the table." Throughout your work, many references but also explicit homages can often be seen. Obviously, in our conversations so far, lots of names have popped up. So today, I'd like to talk about poetry throughout the ages & how it influenced you, & also how you possibly feel indebted to it or want to promote it. Let's begin with the earliest known poet, Enheduanna. How important is she to you & your poetry?

Enheduanna was an Akkadian poet-priestess who lived & wrote in the Sumerian city-state of Ur — a city our Euro-Christian tradition taught us to think of as the left-behind, abandoned, origin of that core patriarchal figure, Abraham, about whom more when we come to speak of the nomadic. The Sumerian materials first became important to me via Charles Olson who pointed out that the big problem with our oh so Eurocentric world-view & its epistemological limits starts with the Greeks & lasts from Plato to World War II, which he sees as a very problematic block-like period in human history that we need to get out of. To do that, we have to look elsewhere, sideways, say, as he also did, to the worlds of the Maya & other indigenous cultures, or backwards, to the world before Plato. And way more interesting than say the pharaonic super-states of ancient Egypt will be the city-states of Sumer; now Olson didn't get too close to Enheduanna, but there is this quote from a letter addressed to him by one of his great friends & lovers, Frances Boldereff, a typographic designer by trade & an independent scholar by passion, suggesting that he should do an anthology of Enheduanna's writings, around the goddess Inanna. Which he never did, however. I have a poem about the painted hands in the Gargas cave in the Pyrénées that I used recently in a performance — this may be the one you refer to — where I cite Olson & then say "What a shame that you didn't do what she suggested."

Actually, if Sumerian culture interested me via Olson & then reading Noah Kramer & others, it's not me who initially developed the focused interest in Enheduanna. To a great extent, it's Nicole who, when we were looking at prehistoric & early works, researched these matters (these *maters*, or "mothers of us all," these women's neglected or disappeared heritage) & found Enheduanna's songs about the goddess Inanna. When she talked to me about how fascinating this material was, I recalled that Jerry Rothenberg had reproduced one of the Inanna songs in his 1969 anthology *Technicians of the Sacred*. That gave us a first access to these songs, & Nicole started her various "vulva" works. Enheduanna was important, because she, as the first poet whose work has come down to us, has this vulva song about Inanna — one of the great Sumerian works. I'm trying to return to this material in a long poem I hope to get done eventually, which would involve as one of its structures sixty-two poems based on the *mes*, those foundational Sumerian divine decrees. So this is material that is very much part of Nicole's & my collaborative thinking & working, even if each one of us does different things with it. But what to me is worth insisting on is that the oldest written poetry we have on record is by a woman. And Enheduanna's poems addressing Inanna talk about the goddess's vulva, i.e. that & everything that has been hidden by this Greco-European phallocentric culture that has held us in its gyno-phobic claws from Plato to our own century, as Olson had suggested. Time for a widening of the world-view.

Enheduanna was a woman, & quite interestingly in our conversations so far, you have always associated the word poet with "she" & "her" (the reader too, actually); this choice of words highlights your willingness to always put female poets into the light. Beyond the legitimate reasons to do so — which you may nevertheless want to address —, I'm curious to know whether you also see a difference in the poetry, in the voices of men & women poets. And have you already given "theoretical thoughts" to queer poetry voices?

I think poetry is a queer voice to begin with. It is this lateral thing, this art that doesn't want to be nailed down into a fixed mode, a fixed thought. Even though a lot of it is, but that's what I'd call bad poetry. Poetry is a queering of the supposedly or pretendedly straight world. It is what gives another angle of vision of a *monobloc*, a cast-in-one-piece culture. Our Western culture has been very bad about this, but that's not the case elsewhere: Native American culture for example always had connections between queerness & shamanism, between all different aspects of the world, in a way a less solidified or singular vision — I compare the latter to erectile tissue, very, no, all-too male stuff. If you remember the performance Nicole & I did in Luxembourg, I was wearing a dress, a robe — Enheduanna's? — (though, obviously, "l'habit ne fait pas le moine," the dress doesn't make the man — or the woman, & is thus only a very, literally, "superficial" way of speaking about gender issues). Though one of the lines in the poem that plays downstairs in the cave & references our work in & with the cave of Gargas, as well as quoting the Olson/Boldereff material already mentioned, says: "He went in a boy & came out a girl."

I personally haven't worked in any scholarly or deep way on queer writers; it always seemed to me that whatever other poets could bring in would be totally great, that they could provide an angle on things I can't or don't need to take on in my own writing. Poetry is open to any & all. The other day I was preparing a tribute to the poet Jack Hirschman, who passed in August, & came across one of his statements that says it all: "I believe that everyone is a poet and that one of the central reasons that I've fought as a revolutionary is to change not only the material conditions of mankind but, in so doing, to liberate that idea — that everyone is a poet — into human consciousness."

Obviously, for my generation, the important early fight was to step back & let women come into their voices more than they had previously. And they have! I have mentioned this a certain number of times when asked to name the most important poets in my generation one should read: a vast number, probably even a majority of them, are women. I had a plan at one moment with Adonis who'd asked me about a possible anthology of contemporary American poets for the Arab world. I quickly wrote down the names of some 30 women poets. Imagine: exclusively women representing contemporary American poetry, translated into Arabic! I do hope I can get to that project at some time.

But that wouldn't be just an in-your-face gesture, because thinking of the great modernist poets who were my daddies, Pound, Olson, all the way up to Kelly, one can see that one of their great modes of expression is the long poem. Epic at that time was already criticized, because you didn't want it to be too much of a war poem. (Maybe the last great war-epic was the Welsh poet David Jones' *In Parenthesis* — even the title already makes a statement about the genre — about World War I.) We should think about Pound's *Cantos* not so much as an epic poem but more as a *long* poem (with a cycle of songs about World War II, or his experience, the so-called Pisan Cantos) though still based on a very male strength, endurance & lifetime engagement.

If you look around now, most of the interesting long poems are by women. For example Diane di Prima's *Loba*, or *The Descent of Alette*, Alice Notley's work inspired by Inanna's descent into the underworld, which is set in the *métro* in Paris! We already mentioned in our first conversation Rachel Blau DuPlessis's *Drafts*, a poem that took thirty years to complete & where any conclusion is excluded by the very notion of "draft." Which reminds me (again!)

of Robert Duncan's idea of a "grand collage," that we also already touched upon — now he was the great queer poet of his generation —, with its interleaved long processes he produced over many years, avoiding the epic as a war story, even if the work includes some of the most powerful anti-(Vietnam)-war poems of the 2nd part of the 20th century. Lyn Hejinian is another poet with several major long poems/sequences. There's also Anne Waldman's 1000-page long *The Iovis Trilogy*, Bernadette Mayer's work, Rochelle Owens work, & so on & so on. The quality of contemporary work in the mode of the long poem by women is amazing.

But it's not that men don't do it: I'm reading right now someone I feel close to, the African-American poet Nathaniel Mackey, whose latest work came out last month: a boxed set of three volumes called *Double Trio*. It's also two interleaved long sequences: *Song of the Andoumboulou & Mu*. You may remember Andoumboulou from the Dogon mythology as described by Germaine Dieterlen & other anthropologists, & here is Mackey publishing a thousand-page poem that takes off from these materials & brings them home here now, deeply enriched. Also interesting is that Nate doesn't use an "I" but rather a "we," it's a multiplicity, a company of people — musicians, thus a band — traveling, on the road. This was a form already breached in another long poem I learned a lot from, Edward Dorn's *Gunslinger*, published from the late 1960s to the early 1970s. It talks about the mythology of the West in a kind of highly comic epic mode where the figure of "I," the narrator, is somebody who fell into a vat of LSD. This plays against the traditional "I" poetry taught by creative writing & at the same time is an epic, not a war epic but a metaphysical shoot-out epic. It's one of the most wonderful, playful poems I know of. It's also very much of its cultural time, that is, very drug-involved: acid in one section, cocaine in other sections … The horse is called "Hi Digger" & is always sitting in a bar rolling joints with his hoofs & saying incredibly Heidegerrian stuff. This poem never really made it to Europe — to the UK yes, some of it was published there, but never to non-English-speaking countries. I tried to get Christian Bourgois to publish it in French; the rights were difficult to get & Ed told me in the end: "Don't do it, the French would never understand it anyway!"

There is incredible richness in the work that is available in the long form & I could just go on for another hour. Of my own generation closest to me are the long works of the English poet Allen Fisher, his magisterial *Place* for one, & then *Gravity as a Consequence of Shape*, & those of the already mentioned Nathaniel Mackey. But among the previous generation's long works, let me just cite the today much neglected oeuvre of Ted Enslin, the 5-volume *Forms*, or his *Ranger*, or his *Synthesis*. All those taught & keep teaching me. Though I may have learned most from Robert Kelly's masterwork, *The Loom*, a 400-page poem from the 1970s. It fascinated & questioned my thinking, mainly because of the narratological solutions it proposed, so different from Olson's or Duncan's ideas of collage as a main structural procedure because its narratology is very much other. But haven't I come off your question a bit there?

You may have, although I do believe the initial query about women voices was very well covered. But what I actually find fascinating is that in every other conversation we come back to the subject of the long poem, which probably indicates I should prepare some more questions about this theme for an upcoming session.

Then I'll address the short poem, given that I speak about the long poem on all other occasions! But you could also suggest you started out by asking about queering... so I'm queering your questions all the time.

Absolutely! Now, getting additional layers of information about the long poem in different conversations is also an interesting way of proceeding. You mentioned Native Americans in your answer, & that was a direction

I wanted to go to as well. I guess your interest for Native American poetry has an element of you standing up for minorities, but also comes out of your interest for languages. In Europe, Native American poetry is only rarely available through translation. Can you speak about how you came to discover it?

It's true that there isn't that much available. It was difficult here & remains very difficult to come to these cultures. Brought up in Luxembourg, my interest in America came from age eight on by reading Karl May — that 19th century romantic novelist whose 72 volumes of "Reiseerzählungen," or travel narratives, of totally invented worldwide adventures recounted in the first person, fascinated young, mainly male, adolescents (& adult males too, come to think of it). Native Americans, Apaches, were core to this literature, & you'd have thought that America was the country of the Indians. And the innumerable Westerns ("cowboy movies," we called them, with the Indians as the bad guys, nearly always) I saw in the *Cinéma de la paix*, my grandmother's movie house in Ettelbruck. One of my childhood friends, René Oth, who for some years lived a few houses up on Avenue Salentiny, had the most amazing collection of toy Indian figures (& some cowboys & soldiers). We used to play long afternoons, even whole days, setting up historical battles — I remember him being as fond of Nikunta, supposedly a Seminole chief, as I was of Winnetou, Karl May's Mescalero Apache chief. He was ahead of me: Nikunta was a historical figure I believe (though I have not been able to verify net-wise, this memory is close to 65 years old), while Winnetou was a fiction. René also had a range of books beyond my Karl Mays on American Indian cultures — which I would borrow & devour. He moved & I lost track of him — though would come across two books he wrote in the 1990s on the history of Native Americans. If I can track him down, I'd love to send him a copy of my book *Winnetou Old*, though that's in no way the kind of *Sachbuch* non-fiction that he writes. I know that even back then I was uneasy about the portrayal of native Americans in those films, & that was at some level due to Karl May who as a German writer claimed critical distance from French & English colonial stances, & so was way more "Indian-friendly" — even if that stance was based on a very romantic Christian religiosity rather than on a political-ideological analysis — & made his fictive "blood brother" Winnetou & the Mescalero Apaches into a truly vibrant culture (though their sworn "enemies," the Kiowa & Comanche, were drawn more or less in the Euro-tradition of bloodthirsty savages). There were also the *Leatherstocking* tales that I devoured at the same time, in late 19th-century German translations, which edited out a lot of Fenimore Cooper's Christian & metaphysical claptrap, leaving lean stories that kept me enthralled with Chingachgook & Uncas. But there may have been one other factor that turned me off cowboy-Indian movies (as against cowboy-cowboy movies). My interest, even back then, was in the cultures, from the clothes to the housing — teepees, pueblos, longhouses, sweat lodges, etc. — to the different cultural ways of approaching & living in the world & especially in nature, to their languages. I had copied out all the Mescalero & other Indian language terms in May's books & tried to create a secret language with them (more details on that in my Batty Weber speech). What I could even if only very minimally perceive of those cultures awed me. And less than a decade after World War 2 the idea that the most glamorous heroic actions were wars against people, whoever they were, simply felt wrong. Just as I never got involved in the wargames the boys my age played against other gangs or villages in the hills & woods behind Ettelbruck — where unexploded German & Yankee ammo from the just-past war was often found, & sometimes exploded, leading to more wounded boy soldiers.

 Then a bit later, I must have been about 13 or 14, I discovered jazz, with my parents taking me to hear Nat King Cole at the Casino in Oostende, then a year later in the same place I heard Ella

Fitzgerald & Louis Armstrong. And suddenly there was another America, a Black America, with blues on the radio & so on. The first 45-rpm I remember buying was Bessie Smith's *Empress of the Blues* — I still have it! — & remember puzzling over what the first song's title meant: "Cake Walkin' Babies Back Home." At 16 or 17 I got my mother to drive me across the border to Thionville for a Ray Charles concert! Then, as I already mentioned at the beginning of the interview, I discovered Black American literature, James Baldwin in my last year in high school, then Langston Hughes & Bob Kaufman. In Paris I also started reading Leroi Jones/Amiri Baraka's work from *Blues People* to *Dutchman* — & was eager to try to meet these poets when I would get to the US.

But coming here — where I am now, talking from, the US of A —, I quickly realized that I was actually entering a predominantly & proud-to-be White America! The Indians had disappeared & Black people were in certain parts of the city you were not supposed to go to. Harlem in the late 1960s & early 1970s was a "dangerous place." A few white friends would go there only to score heroin. You didn't go there for music either anymore; the jazz venues were mainly in the West Village. In my very open university there were just two or three black students. Looking for Native Americans & their culture was even more difficult. I wouldn't meet Amiri Baraka until the late 1980s, never managed to meet Bob Kaufman, & couldn't meet Hughes as he passed 4 months before I reached New York. Jimmy Baldwin I would meet — but on both occasions that was in Paris.

So it did take a while before you could know more about this Native American culture you so much wanted to meet from your early childhood on.

I began coming to a first new understanding of Native Americans via a Robert Kelly text that said that where Native American culture survived most visibly was in the country's toponymy:

you can still hear it resonate in the names of places. But a more active awareness came in very soon after that: in 1969, after I graduated from Bard & moved down to New York City, I discovered a very important book that had come out the previous year: Jerome Rothenberg's anthology *Technicians of the Sacred*, which he would follow a few years later with a purely Native American anthology called *Shaking the Pumpkin*. *Technicians* included the Inanna poems we just talked about, among a worldwide range of early or contemporary tribal poetries, but also a number of Native American works. One reason this culture can now come in or be there has to do with the enlarging of the poetic possibilities in modernism. We already talked about the fact that the poem is no longer that Western form of the sonnet & opens up to wider forms. Oral performance is also something envisioned again for our contemporary poetry. What that meant — & Rothenberg is one of the amazing central figures for this from the mid-20th century to this day (he just turned 90!) — is that you could translate various early poetries, oral poetries, in ways that were previously impossible. A 19th-century anthropologist (& most 20th-century too) would go study Native American culture & suggest: "These people are singing strange & weird songs, that include lots of non-semantic nonsense. Most of the decipherable words are stories relating myths or are connected to making war, or preparing a potlatch, whatever." And he may transcribe the "decipherable" words, or if in the later 20th century, record them with the first tape recorders, but it would essentially be information for other anthropologists. The idea that these songs were part of wider, coherent, multi-level, multi-media active art works was being lost. Jerry & his generation of American poets learned from Pound & Kurt Schwitters that there was this possibility of different forms that could be considered as art just as much as any written European art forms since the Greeks. In *Technicians of the Sacred*, Rothenberg adamantly states in the intro that "primitive means complex." Bang! So Native American poetry is as complex as other art forms & has wonderfully done for centuries what Europeans "invented" in recent decades, things like performance art, the combination of paintings, sound poems, dancing & so on. Dada invented this in Paris or Zurich. Native Americans (& tribal oral artists on other continents) could say: "Hey, we've been doing this for millennia, welcome to the show!" So that was a big opening for me.

As I wrote in the Batty Weber Award speech, when I drove to Colorado in 1989 & met the first Mescalero Apache I ever met — Inés Talamantez, a formidable woman & scholar in ethnopoetics, linguistics & anthropology who passed a few years ago — I gave her all the words in what was supposedly Mescalero Apache from Karl May's books — & none of them was in any way recognizable … So back in the late 1960s, via Rothenberg's & a few rare other anthologies, I began to investigate Native American poetry. That has only grown in importance since. I also mention this in the essay: I found connections, maybe tenuous, I hope not spurious, but there, I think, between the Native American & Luxembourgish linguistic situation — namely, the necessity to write in another language than the mother tongue, in the Native American case because the languages had died out with the exterminated tribes, or had been forbidden to be taught, or were insistently devalued. For Luxembourg it was more peaceful, certainly no ethnocide at work: our native language was downgraded to a basic low or Platt "dialect" while the cultural invaders, France & Germany, imposed their "high" language. So that most Luxembourgish writers feel forced to choose between one of those two. Something that has however been changing in the last decades & there are now quite some writers doing serious work in Luxembourgish.

How to deal with writing in a colonial language is an important topic. I am very taken with the current work of people like Natalie Diaz, a Mojave poet, who thinks & writes about exactly these matters, or the Oglala Sioux poet Layli Long Soldier, whom

I recently asked to read for an event I curated online. There are more connections: in the early 1970s Jerome & Diane Rothenberg went to live on a Seneca Reservation in Upstate New York & worked with Seneca poets & healers as well as doing translations. The concept of "Total translation" was Jerry's idea, a concept proposing that you can now do justice to the incredible complexity of Native American art (& that of other oral traditions) by seeing it as a *Gesamtkunstwerk*, from which you can translate a range or possibly all the elements & recompose them into complex English forms. The classic example of this are Jerry's "Navajo Horse Songs," where he translates the rhythmic & melodic sound elements — i.e. he will sing them —, the semantic elements — in this case the story of how the spirit horses were brought down to earth — as well as the onomatopoeia that connect sound & semantic elements. This was groundbreaking work, even if there are now some Native American poets & post-colonial critics who would criticize him, suggesting that what he is doing is "cultural appropriation" — but then, to my mind, all translation is that to some extent, & all cultures are to a smaller or larger extent creolized! Another way of putting this would be to consider — as Mireille Gansel does — translation as a kind of transhumance.[7] Which also allows for a way of questioning the "appropriation" part of "cultural appropriation" via its root words "proper, property, etc." & thus the concept of private property as overweening & defining cultural value (& root of capitalism) belonging, as it invariably does, to sedentary peoples afraid of nomads & of the very concept of the nomadic. And of course the greatest "appropriators" were the colonial invaders who weren't nomads in any way but just raiders who either grabbed the land to become exclusive sedentary owners or took whatever they could carry back to their sedentary homelands as loot.

7. Mireille Gansel, *Translation as Transhumance* (The Feminist Press at CUNY, 2014. Kindle Edition).

In Stations d'Al-Hallaj, *translated by Habib Tengour & published by Apic Éditions in Algiers, you answer a question on the future of poetry by:* "As long as there is a world & humans, there will be poetry." *So in this continuum of poetry closely tied to the human race, the ancient pre-Islamic* Mu'allaqât *are still relevant some 15 centuries after being written. How have they helped shape your writing language?*

Well, as you know, I have written a fair amount & from varying angles concerning the concept & the necessity of the nomadic, with much of it gathered in the book of essays called A Nomad Poetics. Much of this comes obviously via me thinking about my own nomadicity, at a basic level: leaving Luxembourg, going to Paris, coming to New York, going to London, eventually moving to Algeria & back to America. And beyond the purely geographical *errances*, there is of course the nomadicity of my languages & the decision to write in my fourth. So the concept of changing & moving is core to my life experience. Obviously, it can also fill you with anguish, & there came a moment when I had to think this through. In the early 1970s the concept of the nomadic had wonderfully rich developments in a completely different camp, the one of French philosophy, via the work of Gilles Deleuze & Félix Guattari. Having already spent three years in North Africa & being very interested in North African literature, which pushed me a bit also into looking into Mashreqi literature, I came across these amazing early nomad poems. There was a quasi-Shakespearian sense to them in their culture: the *Mu'allaqât* are both the origin & the perfection of Bedouin poetry. And it so happens that at that moment — it must have been 1977 — my companion of those years, Zahia Matougui, had invited a friend from her London days, an Iraqi scholar. His father had a second-hand bookshop on Al-Mutanabbi Street in Baghdad, so he grew up inside that classical Arab culture & learned much of the *Mu'allaqât* by heart, as core to the Arabic poetry tradition. I was looking at them in a French translation, because I didn't have Arabic.

So he said: "Oh! Let me recite you these poems." By this time I had already found my favorite: Ibn Tarafa — most interesting to me, because his work was the least warrior-like, had a more visionary, outsider quality to it. I've often called him a Rimbaudian poet — though I should really say that Rimbaud was a Tarafian poet.

I told Mohammed that I was interested in translating Tarafa, & he brought me a print copy of the *Mu'allaqât* in Arabic, which I still have. I penciled his word-by-word translation of Tarafa's qasida into that book. Then I started reworking & tried to find a way to bring this into my own poetics, into the poetics of contemporary American writing. That translation was a true transhumance (not just because I started it in Algeria but finished it later in London & published it first here in the US): the first, literal translation made the elegant high-flying Arabic rhetoric into heavy over-richly adjectivized blobs of English rhetoric that felt indigestible, very 19th-century, at best Hugo-ish, or bad Victorian verse. I had to find a way of cutting through these gelled language molasses. It was impossible to directly imitate the very rich & structurally complex form of the qasida; I needed a lighter form that would allow me to cut out some of the *Fleurs de Tarbes*, the rhetorical flourishes & embellishments that no longer worked for our contemporary minds & ears, having lost any *arête*, sharpness, clearness, to use Pound's term. So I went to a further away Occident, a far East: Japan, & decided to use the form of the linked haiku, a kind of two-authors, or better, in this case, an author-translator renga — a form that in its processual working out also linked back (or forward again) to the American modernist William Carlos Williams' three-stepped triadic verse forms. The process of this translation, & then composing Ibn Tarafa's *vita* as an introduction, was one of the great pleasures of my transhumance/translatory life. As it happens, years later, two weeks after 9/11, as soon as the airports were open again, I flew to Naropa University in Colorado to give a talk. It was originally supposed to be on global cultural matters but I decided to focus exclusively on Arab culture (which seemed essential to me right then as part of my work in countering the spreading of anti-Arab rhetoric in the political world) & made the Tarafa qasida the center point of that lecture. In a very practical sense, I had been interested in seeing how these ancient poems worked; why they were so important to such an immense literary tradition, which by the way was completely neglected — as are African traditions — by the Western Europeans & Americans, except for fake Hafiz pearls of wisdom. I just read an article saying that most of the Hafiz books — he's with Rumi the most read Persian writer in America! — are 80 to 90 percent pure invention, fake wisdom.

To me, these early *Mu'allaqât* poems were interesting because they were also totally part of their tribal political culture. Poets could be not only singers, but also leaders of the tribe or going to war in some way or another. Or they could act like Tarafa, just telling the king off: "Fuck you! I'm not going to say what you want to hear & do what you want me to do." Of course that meant he had to die. And he replied: "First fill me with wine, then you can bleed me to death." There are amazing figures in the *Mu'allaqât* of the poet as a cultural center, but also as a counter-cultural center at the same time, exactly what we in our way have been looking for or have been attracted to by the likes of Rimbaud or Walt Whitman & such visionary, ground-breaking, border-crossing poets. So that was important to me. And the fact that I don't know the language well or only have teeny bits of it has also deeply interested me. I love hearing Arabic even though I cannot understand much of it. I love listening to, for example, Adonis reading. I just hear this like a concert in a way & also play with it: *Meditations on the Stations of Mansur Al-Hallaj* that you mentioned earlier was formally interesting in that I found the 40 terms that Al-Hallaj uses in his Sufi teachings, in Arabic, then started to investigate meanings word by word & wrote poems out of each term. To me, this is a way to get, if not into the heart, than at least into the surrounds on a day-to-day basis of a language I do not master.

In a strange way, two days ago, Nicole & I wanted to get brunch but didn't want to go to a diner. A fifteen-minute walk from here gets us to a big Yemeni *quartier*, & I love *phool mudammas*, the great Mashreqi breakfast dish based on crushed fava beans, tomatoes, & olive oil. So we found this new Yemeni restaurant — the best *phool* I've had in ages! — & then went to check out the new shop across the road, where the young lady who was the salesperson turned out to be an Algerian Berber. The owner is Yemeni, so we talked in a mix of English & French, & Nicole added some Tamashek words that she got from translating poems by Berber poet-singers for my anthology. I found a bottle of olive oil clearly coming from Morocco called "Agadir." I decided to buy it — & I'll probably put a photo of the label up on Facebook at some point —, then started asking them what they knew about Agadir. They knew it to be a city, but they didn't know its history, & of course didn't know that I had just published a translation of Mohammed Khaïr-Eddine's book *Agadir*. It was a fascinating encounter. I love being in that multicultural setup, talking food, drink, poetry, language … That's another reason I love New York so much. I can just walk into all these different worlds, they're right here! The world is nomadic, & the nomadic is at my door. I heard the other day that French fascist, Éric Zemmour, who laid it out exactly in one sentence: "*Nous sommes dans une situation où les sédentaires sont agressés par des nomades venus du sud de la Méditerranée.*" I.E., "we (the French) are the threatened sedentary high-culture [only sedentary peoples, of course, can have a high culture] who are being attacked by rabid nomads coming up from the South." That's how he summed up his whole ideology — and unhappily it is an ideology rampant if not yet victorious in too many northern, predominantly white cultures, these United States included. And I thought: "Yes, there we are. Let 'em come!"

5th Conversation

November 13, 2021

In an interview with Orlando Reade about The University of California Book of North African Literature, *you say that if Habib Tengour & you had had 300 pages more you would have ventured into Chad, Niger, & Mali, for example. Even though we can't pretend to talk our way through an unwritten chapter of an already published anthology, what can you share about what you discovered — or were planning to discover maybe — there?*

The answer is complex. Our original manuscript was in fact 300+ pages longer & the publisher forced us to cut back. Our preferred title for the book had been *Diwan Ifriqya* (Ifriqya being the old name for North Africa) — but at the last minute the publisher also had us change that to the *University of California Book of North African Literature*. The reason we didn't do it (go further south), or why it wasn't possible, is that when you use the term "Maghreb," you automatically delimit the geographical area. Maghreb is an Arab word which means "west." That is why I was kidding Habib when I was reading with him in Iowa City a few weeks ago, saying: "We are now in the real Maghreb, the Wild Maghreb! This is the west of your West & where you're from, seen from here, is the Orient." If you go to some of the great Sufi texts, such as *The Occidental Exile* by Shahāb ad-Dīn Yahya ibn Habash Suhrawardi (the one called the "Master of Illumination" — *Shaikh-i-Ishraq*), of which there is a superb French translation by my old, now sadly departed friend Abdelwahab Meddeb (*L'Exil occidental*, Albin Michel, 2005), you'll learn that it is in that Occident that knowledge resides. I did my own writing-through of that Shurawardi text in a prose/poem called *h.j.r.* (Arabic for "exile") in the book of that same name (also reprinted in *Poasis*, WUP 2001). So, seen from the Wild (American) West, Habib's Maghreb becomes the East, the occidental (accidental?) exact place of knowledge.

We stopped going further south because this is a question, not only of pages, but also of languages. The Arab influx comes from the 9th century on, & can be symbolized by Oqba Ibn Nafi, the general who rides as far West as possible, i.e. into the Atlantic on the Moroccan coast, holds his horse, looks out & says: "This is the end." I have a poem where I speak to that & say that he didn't know there was this other continent, another, a Far Maghreb, thus a Far West on the other side called America. Or misnamed America by the stupid Europeans who "discovered" it, thinking they knew everything. Anyway, the South is fascinating & it would have been great to do more on that, because obviously Arab nomad invasions went all over the place. It also becomes more complex culturally, as you have to talk about the Arab slave trade, & the local African cultural traditions when you come to some of those that are totally enthralling (& really need anthologies of their own). I'm currently rereading material on Dogon culture. So of course you could do an anthology of the "Sub-Saharan Maghreb." And both Habib & I are very much drawn in by all those areas, because of their oral traditions.

Now Jerry Rothenberg did a lot of that work in his anthology *Technicians of the Sacred*, laying out the fact that these oral traditions have existed for millennia & millennia & still exist & thrive all over the world. There are untold millennia of oral literature from all around the world, but only a few rather localized centuries of "written" literature. We had to obviously put a limit, borders on what we were doing. In the introduction we defined what the borders of the Maghreb were: from the Kufra oasis to the Atlantic Coast. Mauritania is included in the South. In the North, we added an extra chapter on Al-Andalus, because Spain was once highly cultured when the Arabs & the Berbers were there, a culture that came to an end unhappily the same year Columbus got lost at sea & made landfall in what he called America! That nomadicity was what we could deal with; we needed those limits.

To me, the other cultural way of defining the geography of the Maghreb is to say that it is the area where couscous is the staple food. Once you cross from the Kufra oasis into Egypt, you're more into the favorite fava bean breakfast food I mentioned last time, *phool mudammas*. So you're in the Mashreq! That's another way of thinking about it, which is why I always have a double take when in restaurants I come across "Israeli" or "Near Eastern" couscous: it seems a rip-off, those very white very round large micro-balls that don't look at all like "real" i.e. Maghrebi couscous. Couscous is a North African thing; now of course Jewish immigrants who lived in the Maghreb & settled in Israel will be familiar with it. But when in my grocery shop in America it says on the shelf "Israeli" or "Near Eastern" couscous, I always kind of wonder. You may say that it is a cultural *détournement* that at one level I should be really pleased with, because I love cultural *détournements*, & everything should be totally mixed.

Well, I was indeed thinking about that, given your advocacy for the free circulation of cultures.

Yes, the only way to make things work is by mixing everything up. At the same time, to get away from this silly food-fight, I am very happy that some works of art get taken from our museums to be sent back to Benin & elsewhere. However, I would like very good copies of those pieces to remain, so that we can still see them! Or my real desire on this is that we should, with the Benin people say, make exchanges: you leave those works with us & we compensate you with our best Picassos, de Koonings, Kiefers & so on, then we'll come to look at our things in your country & you come to see your things in our country. As you may know, there is in America right now a lot of discussion in universities on cultural appropriation. It's a very difficult thing, because you can clearly see that people get ripped off. At the same time, my sense is that all culture is appropriation. There is no "purity." Let me quote myself again: "Purity is the root of all evil." I think the way to go about it is more anarchic, a sort of non-violent anarchism that does not proceed by war raids, but rather by completely friendly exchanges, or as a core aspect of Kropotkian "mutual aid." For example, in Native American cultures, you can find shells associated with one specific place on the East Coast anywhere on the continent because they were exchanged for other types of materials. If we could get to an anarchic, friendly exchange economy, you couldn't call it cultural appropriation or rip-off anymore.

Anyway, I am currently reading a wonderful, immense book that I hope will come to Europe soon — oops, it just did —, called *The Dawn of Everything: A New History of Humanity*.[8] It's a deep revision of Western culture, starting with Rousseau's myth of the innocent primitive not knowing much but living very happily, & then agriculture & capital came & everything gets ruined, then kings come & so on. David Graeber is one of the authors & I ran into him at least one or twice when he was the "anarchic director" of the Wall Street demonstrations ten years ago. He was an anthropologist — he passed at 59 last year, three weeks after completing this book with his colleague David Wengrow, an archaeologist. What they're saying is that, looking at the early texts where that whole notion of inequality — a notion very much talked about now — comes from is Europe, a lot of the ideas for equality & freedom actually come from Native Americans. These were great talkers, & when the Jesuits landed, a number of the Native

---

8. David Graeber & David Wengrow, *Au commencement était…: Une nouvelle histoire de l'humanité* (Les Liens Qui Libèrent, 2021).

chiefs & orators were as good as them concerning the subtlety & depth of their analyses, even though they hadn't read the Roman or Greek treaties on speechmaking! If you look carefully at the famous Jesuit records of the discovery of America, Europeans are completely stunned by what the natives tell them: "You're not free, look at the hierarchy you're in," for example. The seriously subversive point made, explored, proven by innumerable examples in the book, is that rather than having developed along the kind of rigid linear unidirectional line that Rousseau, Hobbes, Marx or any of the Westerners describe, humans have been deeply aware & played since prehistoric times with any number of political or cultural possibilities. The main narrative we live under needs to be deconstructed, this "grand narrative" as Jean-François Lyotard would call it, which says that we live in a disaster where Western culture is at the end of its tether, having fucked the planet up so bad that our species may no longer be viable on it. *The Dawn of Everything: A New History of Humanity* is truly an immense book. I was lucky I was sent a copy by Farrar, Straus & Giroux, & it's going to be my reading for the next few weeks. Did we go somewhere near where you wanted to go?

Definitely, because I believe we got deeper into your conception of nomadism, among other things — I tend to think more & more about my questions as mere starting points. We've talked Native American & African cultures, & I thought of getting back to Africa for a while. Last time you mentioned Dogon culture already when you presented a book by Nathaniel Mackey. The other day, when we had a short planning session, I saw in your background a range of books, among which I recognized a title, Kindred. I'm assuming this is the book by Octavia Butler?

Actually no! It's *Kindred: Neanderthal Life, Love, Death and Art* by Rebecca Wragg Sykes. I've only read some of it because there were 10 other books that came at the same time, but it is very interesting. We are at a fascinating moment: it may well be the end of the species

Homo stupidus stupidus. And the anxiety that is here means some people are looking at what happened from a different angle. In this book, there is a lot of new work presented that is being done now on Neanderthal, a species always talked about as "those were the primitives, we beat them up & they died out because they were so stupid." Typical talk for *Homo sapiens sapiens* — as he arrogantly calls himself, & "he" instead of "she" is important here also, as a little parallel with the book we just talked about, *The Dawn of Everything*. What I find totally interesting in this is the fact that it comes now after 50 years of my & Jerry Rothenberg's generations rethinking a number of things, in a way, among which the idea of African or Native American cultures being actually amazingly rich, not primitive — remember Rothenberg's "primitive means complex." Nicole & I just watched two interesting documentaries on Amazonian Indians, one called *Ex-Shaman* by Luiz Bolognesi. It talks about what happened when Christian priests took over & the shaman lost his power in his village. So there's currently a vast amount of new thinking about human & animal cultures. It may be too late... But, importantly so, the relationships between realms — living realms such as animals & plants but also minerals — are being reevaluated completely. Having put the human up there as the *ne plus ultra* of creation was our biggest mistake. The hubris of Western white culture in that sense is absolutely, devastatingly lethal. But we now have the means to think differently. You wanted to go on to lighter things, but here we are at the end of the world! And the poets play a role here. I was looking at some early writings by Charles Olson yesterday, & he is absolutely dead on & totally central. It's strange: in my lifetime I really have a sense that a vast range of things opened up in absolutely new ways, just as simultaneously since 1945 we have lived under the mushroom cloud of possible atomic disaster. The Chinese saying about living in interesting times is right. That's problematic: you really want to live in not-so interesting times!

Although it was the wrong book I was thinking about, the connection to our talk of the one you took out of your library is amazingly spot on. What people may not realize as well is that we all inherit a small percentage of our DNA from Neanderthal, which speaks to the necessity of revising the Western "grand narrative." Let's then go back to Africa.

Yes, let's!

What is your relationship to African literature written in English? I'm thinking for example of Nigerian novelists Chinua Achebe or Wole Soyinka, or of Malawian poet Jack Mapanje.

Mapanje I don't know well, except for some of his prison poems, or dealing with that experience. I may be less close to the literature you mention because of the form, the novel. I have taught Achebe, Nuruddin Farah, & others. I actually met Achebe when he was teaching at Bard College & Wole Soyinka at Albany when he came for a reading, & again, briefly, two years ago in Abu Dhabi. But if you want, yes, there is too much even for a compulsive reader like me, & I have not dealt exhaustively with the novel, as poetry is my mode of functioning & thinking. But there are people in Africa whose work interests me a lot, for example the Kenyan novelist Ngugi wa Thiong'o who went from writing in English back to writing in his native language, Gikuyu. I was with him on an ATA (American Translators Association) panel at the University of Las Vegas some years ago. It was a fascinating event, with me as the assistant & translator for Assia Djebar, the Algerian writer. If I had more time, I'd love to do much more with this literature too. At this point, my wanderings into African literature may go more via oral poetries. Right now, as I mentioned, I'm looking at Dogon material because I have some animal sequences in mind, like some of the *Fox-trails, -tales & -trots* recently published in Luxembourg. I always wanted these poems to include cousin coyote in America.

But also cousin fennec in the Algerian Sahara, & then in Dogon mythology Yourougou, the pale fox. I am 75, & if I had another 75 years … So, unhappily, I will also not get to read all the Southeast Asian material I'd love to read. Those are the limits. "Limits are / what any of us / are inside of," to quote Charles Olson again. It's true that I have not spent much time in Sub-Saharan African. I only did one trip with my first wife to Togo & to Benin, traveling around that area while visiting my parents who strangely enough — but my father was adventurous — worked for two years in Tsevie, Togo, in a hospital the Luxembourg government had financed. Another core experience re Africa happened before I moved back to the US in 1987. A good friend, the Senegalese poet & movie director Djibril Diop Mambéty showed me his film *Touki-Bouki*, & asked me to evaluate the English subtitles that had been done by the British Film Institute, as he was getting ready to show the film in the US at, I think it was, the Chicago Film Festival. Djibril did a running translation (into French) of the original Wolof & I checked against the subtitles. And those subtitles were lousy, so for example, where the main character early on in the film yells "shit, shit!" the BFI translation was something like "oh my, oh my"… So over two days & nights Djibril & I redid the subtitles completely. That was an amazing experience! I wish that Djibril had been able to do more film work, but unhappily, he passed — way, way too early, he was only 53 — in 1998.

So now, unless some great occasion for travel opens up again, I have to stay with the books, listening to Pygmy & other musics: we however now have masses of very enthralling recordings, fortunately.

Maybe then one last question to wrap up our world tour: in the course of our conversations so far, is there a culture that we haven't mentioned & that would mean a lot to you as well?

Yes, & I'm starting to think a lot about it again: that's Caribbean culture. Remember I mentioned that I discovered really interesting literature in French when I was pointed to North African authors, as well as Caribbean authors. In the colonial situation, the French language really got worked over, transformed, so as to fit this non-hexagonal situation. Besides Aimé Césaire, who's the great classic — I was just checking out some of his writing again because of translations Nicole & I are doing —, the one I'm really getting back to & see as a big brother for me is Édouard Glissant. His thinking is a nomadics in my terms. It's about the in-between. *L'Intention poétique*, as well as *Poétique de la relation*, which to me is one of the most amazing books about errancy, exile, & moves between languages. I'm so sorry that when I was teaching at Albany, for whatever reason I never got to meet Glissant, who was teaching at New York University. I would have loved, if we had met 30 years ago, to translate some of his work. Today I can't take on any more translations!

All right, we'll print that very clearly so that everybody understands!

Indeed, I had an email yesterday from Mohammed Bennis, the great Moroccan poet & a good friend, asking me to translate some poems of his for a collaboration with a painter. I had to tell him that I couldn't. There is definitely regret here. Anyway, I am rereading Glissant, because the Caribbean islands are a totally fascinating area. An area of multicultural, transcultural post-colonial thinking that is very rich in so many ways. A place to visit soon, maybe …

6th Conversation

December 6, 2021

There's a subject we cannot avoid in these conversations, & that is translation. In *Arabia (not so) Deserta*, citing the example of a contemporary Czech poet whom you don't name, you write: "Bad translation can kill a poet for a whole generation in a country or for a culture." As we talked a lot about the job of the poet, let's focus for this session on the job of the translator. Rather than starting with your job as a translator — we'll obviously come to that —, I'd like to get a few thoughts from you about your experience of being translated. My experience with you is that you do not make things easy for translators in your poems. But the fact is that you can be very cool when it comes to giving feedback. If you're satisfied with the flow, you just make a few remarks (always to the point, that is) on idiomatic expressions that could be used for example, & that's pretty much it. So what do you consider really important when someone translates you? How would that be different from you translating someone else?

Well, my sense is that it would be about the same. To me, a good translation is in a way always the most literal, the one that stays closest to the original that is the most accurate. I really loathe it when a translation prettifies the original. This happened to me at some point when somebody translated me into French. My English, the way I break lines, the way I play with very fast line changes, doesn't work very well in French. I prefer it to be *holpereg*, as they say in Luxembourgish, inelegant, rather than a smooth nothingness. I learned that when I was still translating toward French, very much in relation to trying to translate Kerouac's *Mexico City Blues*. In the book, Kerouac is listening to bebop, blues, his is a very jazz-inflected language; actually he breaks the language, cracks the lines, moving rhythmically down the page as he feels the rhythmic breaks.

(Not that there are no formal constraints: he wrote those poems into a relatively small-size notebook & used the page of the notebook as the overall length limit of each chorus.) Now, throughout the choruses, there are interjections, scatting & so on. And of course, when you try to put that into French, the French language just tries to kick you in the ass: "No, no, no, no, you're ruining me, stop this! I have a structure that needs to be kept, because I'm a classical kind of girl." It seemed to me essential to do something in French that was similar to what was being done in Kerouac's English, as those were the rhythms that make for the pleasure poems give. This leads to the necessity of violence being inflicted on the syntax, for example, with breakages, repetitions … & doing it by ear, so that you could get a pleasant bebop-py sound structure, or at least a sound structure that worked rhythmically. That to me was a big lesson in how to translate & in how I would want to be translated. Again, my long experience with translating Celan is that you translate word by word.

A couple of days ago, the American poet Robert Bly died — & I know one shouldn't speak bad of the dead. He was a very public poet, reading in a sarape or poncho, trying on a sort of fake shamanic role. Jerry Rothenberg & Robert Kelly started the concept of "deep image," which they let him (& a few other poets) use as Jerry & Robert thought they had done with that idea all they could. Bly came to read at Bard in 1969, & it was an odd experience. Robert Kelly didn't want to deal with it, so I was kind of in charge. I took him to his room & he took his synthetic jacket off, removed his tie, then threw his poncho over his drip-dry nylon shirt & — became the shaman … When we were in the bar afterwards, drinking, I said: "Robert, I looked at some of your Baudelaire translations. There's a line there that I don't think is at all what Baudelaire wrote." He said: "Oh! You know, I don't really know French." Then I said: "Well, in the Rilke translation, I wanted to ask you…" — "Oh! I don't really know German." Then I knew he was faking it, at least in his translations. That kind of work should better be called "Imitations" (as Robert Lowell actually did call a book of his "reworkings" of poems by other poets). You can read this little story in my Facebook post from yesterday, because my old friend Stephen Kessler from those Bard College days wrote a piece, a sort of both friendly & appreciative obit that is also critical, on Bly for the *Los Angeles Review of Books*.

What I have said & repeated over the years — you can find this in many of my published texts — is that if a poem in translation reads, looks, sounds easier or smoother than the original, then it's a bad translation. A translated poem can only be as complex or even complicated — & often has to be even more so — than the original.

Just to get back to your French translations, & in particular the Kerouac one: you said you had to perform some violence on the grammar, so how was that received? Because Christian Bourgois, the publisher, is a rather prominent one in France.

I think it was well received. But that's not all due to me. Remember the people who were translating William Burroughs & Allen Ginsberg at that time were my close friends Claude Pélieu & Mary Beach. They did Burroughs's cut-up novels, which was very complicated: Mary built a kind of a card system where all recurring sentence-fragments were noted, in order to remember how they had already translated them when that specific cut-up fragment would return later or elsewhere. Readers who would have gone to read Burroughs & some of his cut-up works like *Nova Express* & probably some Ginsberg, would come to Kerouac's poetry & find it very readable, because the jazz rhythms & so on worked. So I didn't get any bad reception for the Kerouac; in fact, the book (the first two-volume Christian Bourgois edition of 1976) sold out & had a paperback edition (10/18 #1288) in 1978, & then came out again from Christian Bourgois in a single-volume edition in 1994. I have since learned that Collection Points, part of Le Seuil, reprinted it in 2006, but only the French — & did so without asking me about reprint rights, etc. That way they did not have to pay me either. As I was in the US I only found out about this edition recently by chance … (Just as I found out now, March 2022, as I am subediting this book, that Gallimard will republish *Mexico City Blues* in April in their prestigious *Poésie* paperback collection — again, without informing me.)

What I see as essential for poetry in translation are bilingual editions, with original poems & translations on facing pages. That way you can see that one of the things my translation does is to be as close as possible to the original in terms of the layout, in terms of the page. I believe this is core, because modern & contemporary poetry invents its own forms as it unfolds on the page. And the translator has to use that, because this is how the poem moves & works. So I think French readers, even if not reading the English version, if they see the poem on the facing page, say to themselves: "Ah, yes! This is how it works in English." Thus not being too upset about the nasty things I did to their language!

Coming back to your comment on what a good translation should be: in Peter Cockelbergh's Pierre Joris: Cartographies of the In-Between, *there's this essay by Marjorie Perloff where she writes about a Celan poem called "Vom Anblick der Amseln," comparing your translation to the one by Heather McHugh & Nikolai Popov. She says that their translation features a nice, melodic flow, where you effortlessly understand what the poem is about, whereas your translation keeps what you call Celan's "oddities of word construction." That's very consistent with what you said indeed. Now we talked once about questions I had about Habib Tengour's French translation of your* Meditations on the Stations of Mansur Al-Hallaj. *I'd like to quote part of your answer: "What you write about translation is rather accurate: translating my multilingual puns & play on words is not only difficult but almost impossible. But I myself have always argued for translation to show these difficulties/impossibilities by its very stiffness or inelegance — rather than erasing them to create a very/too 'readable' surface in the language of the translation, at the cost of oversimplifying the original. Thus the translation points a finger (accusatory or explanatory or...?) at the original, suggesting that one needs the other (& the other needs the one)."* Could you maybe build on this?

Ah, let me link the last things I said about bilingual editions to Celan: I have always insisted on publishing my Celan translations in bilingual facing-page translations from *Breathturn* in 1995 to *Memory Rose Into Threshold Speech* in 2020, & I have written relatively explicitly about this, in the sense that I have been known to claim — maybe extravagantly, but I'll do it again & again! — that there is no original text, & there can't be, because language is not original. Language is already a translation. Simply think about neuronal activity/transmission/memory, etc.: what we're doing is translating! So a poem or piece of writing is a translation into another mode via this other translation that is language. Then, if you want to look at it from the point of view of an actual piece of writing, try to locate the "original" poem? Is it the handwritten note in the poet's notebook? Is it the second, the third, or the fourth draft, adding, subtracting, taking things out? Then the poem gets published in a magazine, among other poems by other authors. That too is the poem, or "a" poem. Then two years later it appears in the poet's next slim or not so slim volume, nestled here among other poems by that author, arranged in very specific ways & thus part of another consistency — or maybe, of a constellation (& if we take Mallarmé seriously when he says "Nothing / will have taken place / but the place / except / perhaps / a constellation" we can see the individual poem as one atom-star in the wider figure of the molecule/book/constellation). Later it may end up in a *Collected* or *Complete Poems* edition, where all of a sudden it's on page 677 of 1,500 pages; that makes it a different work again, right? Because the context is different.

On top of that, you have all the public readings the poet has given. These are as important in a way as the printed version. Each & all of which "apparitions" change the poem, making it somehow different from itself. And further you have the actual & possible translations into other languages! Very complex & rich. Take a Celan poem — which will be & sound & vibrate as a different poem if translated into, say, English or Arabic or Mandarin. The poem is really the accumulation of all these instances. It's again that old conundrum: it's "both and" & not "either/or." In our culture we always look for "the one," the original. But it doesn't exist; it's a fantasy.

It's therefore important to think of the work in those orders of change or instability, & that helps you get away from ideas like "the greatest poet of this or that." It also puts the translator, who as you know is often in a very secondary place in the literary canon, into a different light. Translators have been fighting for decades & decades to get their names on the covers of books, & this is a major fight. You usually have to look somewhere inside the book to know who did the work. It's good to think of such processes as more democratic, more communitarian. In my little piece on Jack Hirschman in the magazine *Cæsura* that just came out this week, I mention that he called himself a communist. This shocked Americans. And I suggest that it's not shocking at all, because for people of his & my generation (not in America but in Europe, & even more so South of Europe) this was a badge of honor. If you now go to the word "common" in "communism," you reach "the commons": open spaces of shared information & knowledge, & that's what translation is in that field. I also speak about those poets who don't translate because of the importance of their little *nombril*, or whatever little dirt gathered in there they stare at & make poems about. That's why I stopped teaching creative writing, as we mentioned in our first session. Quoting William Burroughs, I always told my students: "I ain't innerested in your dirty old condition." Actually, this was one of the two quotes on top of my curricula! The other one was by Arthur Rimbaud: "Je est un autre." Translation as a teaching & learning method was always way more important & useful to me than so-called "creative writing" — & I often had students study Clayton Eshleman's wonderful book on the subject, *Novices: A Study of Poetic Apprenticeship*.

Translating from a language requires an intimate knowledge of it at all levels. Maybe this technical question is to the former professor who turned creative writing courses into translation classes: how do you keep fit for translation? Are there exercises that help you shape your brain for the task? Because I can imagine the brainteasers in Celan's poetry cannot be solved without some "language athlete training."

Official America claims itself a monolingual country. Which it isn't, because of course Latinos & immigrants enrich it with lots of other languages, while the hidden roots of the great variety of native languages are inscribed all over the toponymy of the continent. If you come to New York & wonder why one of those five boroughs is called "Manhattan" — well, just look it up, in a book or on Google, & you'll come to its native roots & etymologies. But in the end, unhappily, the still predominant WASP (White Anglo-Saxon Protestant) ideology & its hidden or visible white supremacy roots demand that English be the only language (even if, in a place like NY, the government issued voting bulletins, say, are in at least 4 or 5 languages). People's high school year or two of French or German is traditionally very bad or totally forgotten a couple of years later. So in academia when teaching translation as modes of creative art actions, my attempt was to expand the notion of translation: you can translate anything from anywhere into something. You don't know French but you love Baudelaire because you've read some English translations? Well, now go & find a poem you don't have in English, read it aloud in French & translate it homophonically. That is, hear & write down the English words that you get out of the semantically not understandable sound. Look at Louis Zukofsky's really great book translating Catullus from Latin purely by homophonic means: that's one way to go.

Strangely enough, yesterday, on Facebook, Kazim Ali, a very well-known American poet of Indian descent, talked about some paintings of his. He has a new book coming out involving writing & painting. I sent him a note saying: "Hey, Kazim, do you remember coming to my translation seminars with these huge paintings?" They were visual translations of a piece of writing. I have always let the students work with whatever they wanted, as long as it wasn't their belly buttons. Of course, all of that is good to learn, even if you know little of a language: you can explore it; play with it. You may not become the best translator if you only have enough Spanish to read the menu in the local Mexican restaurant, of course. But it doesn't matter, because it gives you a start with the language. Then you can go on from there & dig in deeper if the Spanish or whatever language poetry hooks you. Again, I would explain to my students that it was essential to learn at least one foreign language well — preferably even one outside the linguistic group of your mother tongue, thus Arabic or Japanese if you were French or English — & come to understand its structure & syntax, its word-formation-modes & etymological mycorrhizal root system. This is important because it teaches you that word & object ("les mots et les choses") don't belong to each other, don't stick together in some kind of obvious or "natural" sense, & that is something essential to learn & study when you want to become a poet. As the French linguists called it, "l'arbitraire du signe."

Back to translation: I have always intensely disliked people who translate from a dozen languages, eleven of which they don't know, via other people or via some sort of crib-help. Robert Bly, whom I mentioned earlier, did most of his translations via already existing translations. He just Bly-ified them. I only ever did two translations from languages I don't really know. One is Danish:

I translated two poems by Inger Christensen for the *Millennium* anthologies. I also did this a couple of times with Arabic: we already mentioned Ibn Tarafa, & I also did it when my friend Safaa Fathy asked me to translate her book. In that case I said: "I don't really have enough Arabic. I really need to work very closely with you." And she said: "Yeah, cool. But here is a French translation as well as some English versions of it." I worked with those & would tell Safaa: "How come that word in French is this one, & this other one in English? What is the word in Arabic?" She'd then go to the Arabic, & we'd start talking about where the word came from. That process is truly not my favorite for translating, but it was important to get Safaa's book out quickly, as it was based on the Tahrir Square revolutionary days.

Actually, my question also came from an anecdote you mention in Arabia (not so) Deserta, *the story of the bikini in Nabile Farès's book,* Le Champ des oliviers. *You explain that he uses the word "bikini" twice in the same sentence, once even in capital letters: "Siamois II remet ses frusques. Un bikini grandeur majuscules: BIKINI. Un tricot de peau assorti aux sourcils: broussailleux." And you go on explaining that you found out this was a homophonous allusion to the derogatory French word for a North African, "bicot." In order to do that, you had to dig pretty deep & find an interview where Farès actually explained it. The anecdote is fascinating because it leads to the question of where one should stop. When do you allow yourself to stop digging when you're a translator?*

It's a difficult one. It depends on how much energy you have & what you want to do. If the poem reads well, & you look at the original & say: "Well, this is as good as I can do, I looked at everything I could get my hands on," then you let it go. I've said so even in relation to my Celan translations: translation is always an open *chantier*; I could always go back. A recent example: I had finished the final volume of Celan's early poems & sent it to the publisher; it was being processed. Then I was in Paris with Celan's son Eric & Bertrand Badiou having lunch in a Japanese restaurant, talking of course about Celan, & Bertrand all of a sudden said: "Oh! There's something I just found out." In the "Todesfuge," there are these words: "er greift nach dem Eisen im Gurt." We always thought this "Eisen" was an iron rod to hit somebody with. But in fact Bertrand found out that this is a reference to another use of that word in Karl May & other writers: a *Schießeisen*, a revolver, abbreviated *Eisen*. That made sense! I immediately sent an email to my publisher in New York asking to please change that one word. Mistakes get also pointed out over time. So translation is indeed an open *chantier*.

An open chantier *for readers too then. If the one needs the other & the other needs the one, as we saw earlier about the link between original & translation, readers just can't read passively. How can you persuade them that they have to be active, that a translation is just one version of a poem? Are bilingual versions the solution maybe?*

Essential for poetry, as I explained at some length above. Of course you can't do that with 400-page novels. For poetry, I think it's essential. I always insisted on bilingual versions for my poetry translations, although I didn't always get it. Corso & Kerouac were, Celan of course as well. It doesn't work in our 800-page anthologies or even in the *Habib Tengour Reader*, because that would create both physically & financially unwieldy books. But for poetry you need doubleness: it will allow you to look with two different eyes. Bring one in focus, as the other looses some focus. Robert Duncan often talked about his two eyes looking in different directions, & how that was core to his processes. In poetry you shouldn't have a single focus point. Things are always at an edge where they can slip into something else. To get back to Heather McHugh & Nikolai Popov cited by Marjorie Perloff, they published a book called *101 Poems by Paul Celan* with only their English translations.

These "translations" run down the page like generic current American lyric poems. The translators didn't respect any breaks in Celan's architecturally so carefully constructed poems in which line breaks, indents, & word breaks are essential, & as Marjorie writes, those translations read totally smoothly. A reader who first meets Celan's work via these "translations" cannot help it but think: "Oh, these are lovely Paul Celan poems — I understand them without much problem, lovely metaphors, rich images." No. These are Heather McHugh's versions of some Celan poems — made into easily digestible treats. But a Celan poem is not a treat! It is something tough, adamantine, chiseled, they are complex rock-like structures, with deep geological features & fissures & into which you have to dig down, investing time & energy to come to an understanding of the poem. Celan himself is very clear about this. In general terms, as I keep repeating over & over, when a translation is a better, more easily understood read than the original poem, then you know it's a bad translation. It's not a translator's job to make a poem that has its own difficulties easy all of a sudden.

This is not to claim that there is only one way of translating poems — we have already mentioned homophonic translations or Lowell-style "Imitations," & there are of course a vast range of further often playfully explorative ways of moving between & through languages. But essential for me is that the translator has to indicate what his/her method is, & present the original poem-score parallel to the translation so that the reader can at least visually & rhythmically experience the original poem.

7th Conversation

December 17, 2021

In our little literature world tour, you already mentioned Fox-trails, -tales & -trots, *recently published, when talking about animal connections between the Luxembourgish fox & its cousins coyote & fennec. Since you said in our preliminary talk today how you recently made yourself a nice* Schmier, *a piece of bread with apple compote, let's maybe focus on this specific Luxembourgish book, in order to understand how you conceived it, built it — which of course leads to the more general question of how you conceive books, striking a balance between essays & poetry or between already published & non-published works.*

For this book, it's relatively specific, because it was my first book in English in Luxembourg in a very long time. I wanted to put together material, be it poetry or prose, that had some relevance to Luxembourg. Indeed some of the work had been published before. The early fox poems date from the 1970s, they first came out in a small mimeograph edition by poet & peasant press in 1974 under the title *A Single-Minded Bestiary*, but were never reprinted in some later volume of selected poems. So I saw them as central because of the figure of the fox, the *Renert* in Luxembourg. But also, in a way that may not be obvious, that sequence was meant to show why I, *e gudde Lëtzebuerger*, left & how I did it & justified it. Namely that I was not a reluctant immigrant exiling myself to America in order to get a job with hopes of making it & becoming rich, but rather because I needed to go live in that country & its rich cultural mixes as I had decided that theirs was the language I would become a writer in, so I had to go … & at the same time I carried Luxembourg *um Bockel*, on my back. The figure of the fox was important to me from early on; one of the poems featured in the book shows it standing in the corner of the room having taken on the shape of an old grandfather clock. That is an actual dream I had at my grandparents' Asselscheuer farm as a very young boy, thus an actual linkage to childhood. Of course that has to do also with hunting, as my father was a hunter & I spent a lot of time with him in the forest as a kid — thus the poem about seeing mother fox & her young ones playing. Then there is the memory of having my *Ettelbrécker Bomi*, my father's mother, recite to me the opening Canto of our national epos, which she knew by heart, & teaching me the opening stanza; much later reading the *Renert* myself, & in high school, of course, Goethe's *Reineke Fuchs*. I remember always preferring the Luxembourg version to the High German classic Goethe, specifically because of the strong oral aspect of our Renert, where the various animals come from specific places in the country & speak with their local accents — a fascinating addition, widening, enrichment by Michel Rodange of the *Hochdeutsch* classic. And which may have been something that prepared me too for my later encounters with live oral literatures & ethnopoetics. More strangely, when I was able to acquire a first edition — 1872 — of the Luxembourg *Renert*, I saw to my great surprise that the publisher was one Jean Joris, who turns out to have also been the uncle of my grandfather Joseph Joris … a tribal story for sure!

After I left Luxembourg & moved to America, I came across the figure of Coyote in a range of Native American mythologies, where he is such a central presence. This coyote is of course the same kind of outsider figure, a rebellious misfit & trickster as *de Renert*. The added, nearly Loki-like aspect of coyote as shape-shifter immediately struck me & linked those animals — they are cousins & can commingle in any way imaginable. I mentioned that early on I read Ed Dorn's *Gunslinger*; all of a sudden an idea came to me: the fox, exiled by the king, has to leave his country & slips as a blind passenger aboard the *Santa Maria*, to disembark in America & meet up with his cousin coyote, & they have all kinds of adventures.

That's when I wrote those early short fox poems in London, & thought for a moment that maybe I could go on writing a new fox-epos. But things happen; other stuff, including life & travel, interfered. In London, I once drove back home from teaching at the University of East Anglia through Tooting Commons at 2 or 3 in the morning — & there was this fox right there enjoying the moonshine in the middle of the commons in the middle of the city. That was in the 1970s, a decade that witnessed the fox's return as he/she was becoming an urban creature again. Then just 3 or 4 years ago, I was in London for a conference on Jerome Rothenberg & Eric Mottram, staying near the University of London, on Russell Square. It was in a building along that Square that I studied for my MA with Eric Mottram, at the Institute of United States Studies in the early 1970s. As we came out on the street at dusk to go to dinner, we saw a fox crossing the street, leaving Russell Square, to go wherever it did — right there, & very much at ease, in Central London! All of that made me conscious again of those early works, so when the idea for a book published in Luxembourg came up, I decided to work with the connection to the fox, to make that one of the threads. Also, at one point, back in the 1980s, still thinking about my possible fox & coyote epic, I did some research on the European fox-tale traditions, & wound up translating some medieval materials, a kind of erotic version written by monks.

That's "A Retelling of the Story of Renart & the She Wolf" featured in the book, right?

Yes. This came out first in Jerry Rothenberg's ethnopoetics magazine, *WchWay 5/New Wilderness Letter 12*, in 1984. So the fox material became central to *Fox-trails, -tales & -trots*. In fact, right now, one of the threads that winds its way through the next largish poem-assemblage — though I don't know if I'll ever finish it — is the fox doing this nomadic geographical wanderings/wonderings again &

meeting up with the coyote of course, but also with his North African cousin, the fennec. The first night — it was in the fall of 1976 — I drove into the Sahara Desert, I saw a fennec caught in the car lights & without thinking twice addressed him or her as "Evening, cousin!" The fox is clearly my totem animal. I actually discussed it again this past Sunday (December 12, 2021) at our New York celebration of Jerry Rothenberg's 90th birthday: he is still a member of the Beaver Clan of the Seneca, & I said that the fox & the beaver may belong to separate clans, but are very, very closely allied. In that sense, I am a member of the Luxembourg Renert clan! Wonderfully enough, probably the next movie my son Miles will direct & for which he wrote the original script is called *The Hunter and the Fox* & has a strong magical fox figure at its center. He made me a nice fox stamp for father's day — an image I'll eventually have tattooed on my right forearm, facing the *h.j.r.* in Arabic script — هجر — on my left, thus exile & fox will strengthen both my arms.

Now, when I put those poems & translations together, these fox poems didn't make for a big book, & I thought that I had also been writing a lot of prose dealing with my early days in Luxembourg, mainly for Corina Ciocârlie's *Tageblatt* literary supplement & anthologies. I had never published them together, although I had started gathering them in a dossier, for some sort of future autobiography. But then I thought it would be interesting to couple some of these with the fox poems, because of the direct relationship to Luxembourg; then I thought of the little essay, "Nimrod," about my father, both a healer & a hunter, & which I published first in *Samizdat* & then in *Justifying the Margins*. Things simply began to arrange themselves, calling back & forth from one to the other, creating an evolving shape. Of course, I had to also include the one poem I wrote in Luxembourgish — & which is set in New York's Central Park — as a sort of conclusion, uniting Luxembourg & New York. It's always the same process: I gather material & try to organize it in such a way as to create a coherency that is not circular (i.e. closed in on itself) but that radiates beyond its own atomic & molecular structures. I have never arranged a book in some kind of alphabetical or chronological order, unless the chronology is in some way part of the poems. This goes back to working on late Celan: in those last four volumes he becomes ever more what I call a "serial poet." Which in turn for me rhymes with what I learned in the late 1960s from American poets such as Jack Spicer, Robin Blaser, or Robert Duncan, who tried to eschew concentrating on the single poem — which invariably involves the old idea of the single masterwork poem, like Eliot worked at all his life long — but rather aimed at working on ongoing sequences anchored in a daily alchemical movement of transformation open to the outside & its changing influences. Robert Duncan had several such serial poems, or sequences going on simultaneously over many years (the "Passages," for example, or the "Rimes"); then in his books he would braid these sequences together, interspersed with other poems, in ways he found structurally or architecturally relevant (I had first misspelled this word as "architexturally" — a creative typo or misspelling Duncan would have relished & left in the poem, had it occurred in a poem). Spicer's poems are composed as "books," not individual poems. Just as I read Celan's late works as completely sequentially coherent from *Atemwende* on. The book is the unit, rather than the individual poem. The whole book is in a way four sentences, as each sequence is a sentence. So this has always been with me when the time came to structure my books.

Of course, sometimes, this doesn't work, because the daily writing habit also produces dailinesses that are not necessarily sequential. I'm seriously open though to playing around with any of these formal procedures. Another little book I did, in Luxembourg also — *The Book of U* —, was basically all poems dealing with or having some connection to cormorants. These came from walks I took in the morning here along the Verrazano Narrows, where there are lots of those birds. And I thought to myself that I already knew something about them. In fact, there are a couple of poems I wrote that include cormorants when living on the Pacific, in Encinitas, near San Diego. They became fascinating animals to me qua birds, I marveled at the way they flew like straight arrows just above the water, how they landed & took off, how they congregated in small or vast colonies, sharing trees with white egrets, creating that so valuable substance — for humans! — guano or bird shit. I wanted to link to that reality of the cormorant in front of my eyes, rather than make it into a literary metaphor, as John Milton did in *Paradise Lost* where the cormorant, perched on top of the Tree of Life, is a stand-in for Satan, symbolizes greed, and spies on Adam. Coleridge called himself a "library cormorant," — an image revived a few years ago by the American poet Susan Howe, & which I can indeed feel in accord with.

So I began reading up on cormorants in various cultures, & suddenly remembered that, as a very young poet, I had met a couple of them in Basho's work. I went back to my old H.R. Blyth Haiku volumes bought in 1965 & which I hadn't opened in some years, located the two Basho haiku involving the cormorant, & decided to do a playful homophonic translation of the Japanese. So there was suddenly an open-ended sequence of poems small & tight enough to fly in direct formation from one to the other end of the book, while however also allowing open-ended side-flights or -escapes. I'm more interested in such coherent-incoherent sequences than in the "greatness" or "perfection" of individual poems. You can connect this process of writing with everything I said about translation, the multiplicity of the text, or with my "purity is the root of all evil," the search for the single perfect object or the single absolute, i.e. a god-head of some order — but we know he/she/it is dead, because that form of absolute never existed in the first place. Always the many, never the one.

There's also one link that you haven't mentioned but that I believe is pretty natural. We've talked about it a couple of times already, & it's the collage. A book could be also a coherent & playful collage, in a way.

Indeed, collage is one of the possibilities when building cohesive assemblages. It teaches us that the strangest & most distant objects can not only fit together on the same page, but by their juxtapositions create something new that gives new insights.

The fox poems from 1974 that you have republished in Fox-trails, -tales & -trots *come from the collection called* A Single-Minded Bestiary, *where one can also find the wolf, the genet, the zibet, even the fennec already… Last summer, in a conversation, you mentioned to me that you have a special relationship with spiders. Is your connection with other living species linked to your desire to promote a world in which humans would not be the pinnacle?*

This is becoming ever more central for me now. Like any white European, I was groomed in our society through family & school, through the whole religious insistence, to believe that the white male is the top of creation & that this is both the great insight of & is proofed by the so-called "enlightenment." This has been so for some — even if only a few — Eurocentric centuries. In your family, you "honor" woman, from one's mother on down including your sisters, but somehow, you the male, are the top. Even if parents love everybody equally. I was brought up that way, even if in a very loving family. The fact that I was able to do what I wanted to do, even when it went against the "normal" ways of the bourgeois family, is connected to that, no matter how much it is also due to the very liberal & open-minded thinking of my father. I could leave when I needed to leave because I had that position of the first-born male. Given that I didn't come to America to become a successful business man, I obviously had fallen off the wagon of traditional expectations somewhere in Europe already. Maybe even already in Ettelbruck when I left the church & went to have *apéritifs* instead, communion now becoming a glass of wine to sip & a book to read. Or when I stayed home a lot because I was bored with my high school friends & preferred to get lost in tons of books. Whatever it is, I began moving elsewhere than where I was supposed to. Happily my parents were okay with what I was doing, though obviously it took a lot of discussions. Coming to America & discovering how starkly visible & simultaneously mythologized this idea of white superiority was & where it led, & beginning to see what this, the so-called greatest democracy in the world, was in the reality of its semi-hidden underbelly — I came here in the late 1960s when there were plenty of inner-city riots —, I began thinking about these questions. I came here hoping, if you remember, that I would be able to see Native Americans & connect à la Karl May. But what happened instead is this stop we mentioned earlier, because of an accident in Two Guns, Arizona: we were on Navajo land but I never saw a single Navajo, just white cowboys looking strangely at our long hair ...

Another learning experience on that subject was reading philosophy. In Europe there came a certain relativization & critique of that old European superiority narrative from the likes of Foucault. I had *Les Mots et les Choses* with me when I came to New York in August 1967, as well as Derrida's just published *De la grammatologie*. Deleuze would become even more important for me over the next decades & I would teach *Mille Plateaux* well into this century. At another differently & more directly radical level, I had had the immense good luck of meeting James Baldwin in Paris in the mid-1960s, just when I started reading his essays (my copy of *The Fire Next Time* is signed October 1966) — & continue to do so to this day. So I began building awareness, which Jerry Rothenberg's *Technicians of the Sacred* expanded with insights about what had happened to Native Americans & where the surviving tribes were at now. I began to have a critical vision of the American project: what was my position as a white male there? That question of white privilege is still very acutely there today, as the institutional racism embedded in the history of this country is coming to the fore once more. When I left New York in the early 1970s & moved to London, this questioning awareness of the consequences of white colonialism kept growing. South Africa was beginning to see upheaval, & I got involved in marches, etc. During the late 1970s living & working in Algeria, I had time to read up on anticolonial literature, from Frantz Fanon on out. For 13 years, my life companion was an Algerian scholar.

I don't know exactly why what happened to me happened to me. But instead of doing the expected, i.e. of going to medical school in Paris, sowing my "wild" oats & then going back to Ettelbruck to open a medical or dental cabinet & settle down with wife & children, something else happened to me. This wasn't simply something happening to my mind, it was the world falling in on me & doing the job it should do on anyone of us if one really starts looking around & poking behind the pretty self-satisfied surfaces we are surrounded by &/or consciously surround ourselves with. When I came back from Algeria to London in 1979, I got a job co-editing *Al-Zahf Al-Akhdar*, the Libyan Revolutionary Committee's weekly paper. It was an Egyptian radical journalist, Zainab Abbas, who had started it & hired me on. Our idea was that this small English-language publication the Libyan government was financing could eventually be expanded beyond Libya & its concerns (though we already covered much of the so-called "Third World") to become a Europe-based platform for writing & thinking about postcolonial situations, from the point of view of African, North African, Asian, etc. peoples rather than as seen through the eyes of European journalists. My role in there was more that of the translator, rewriter, though I also worked at expanding, adding articles, & so on. Deeply fascinating work: on one day I may be writing an editorial explaining some aspect of the revolutionary direct democracy process as proposed in Qaddafi's *Little Green Book*, while the next day I may be synthesizing a range of documents showing the lethal influence the Nestlé corporation has in selling its "glamorous" modern products to Africans. That was very important & essential to my formation, my working inside of & with these & similar matters & materials — even if I walked out one day because of my total disagreement with how Qaddafi (who was at that point however not yet the complete paranoid dictator he would soon become because of his own limitations & under unbearable US pressure) was treating Palestinians who had sought refuge in Libya.

The last big piece of writing I did in that context was a 100-page political pamphlet called *Global Interference*, detailing the US government's interference in third-world politics, of course with special reference to Libya, but expanded to the rest of the world too. It came out with, as co-author (though I wrote it in one week all by myself), one of the celebrity old-time anti-colonial English parliamentarians, which allowed us to launch the book in a p.r. room of the House of Lords. That was in 1981. When 7 years later I was a visiting writer at the Iowa International Writers Program, a proud librarian showed us the new early computerized systems linking the university libraries, & after my name was typed in, the results showed that while there were many, many copies of *Global Interference* all over the country, there were, sadly, many fewer of my poetry books that popped up in that search. That was astounding & freaked me out somewhat later on when the FBI had to do some research to see how clean I was before granting me a green card & then later a passport. Strangely enough I recently found out that *Global Interference* has meanwhile been translated into Arabic & is taught in, at least, Iraq.

Returning to America in 1987, all these matters kept being present, boiling up, exploding in our faces in any number of ways. Today, 30 plus years after my return, we're still — or again — or anew — at a moment when what we are living through, what we are witnessing, may be the last two years of American democracy. There's a good chance that the fascists will take over or try another coup by 2024 … Now I can't remember where we started out!

We started by mentioning your connection to animals & other living beings, rather than humans.

Oh yes! There's one interesting thing philosophy-wise, 30 years after the French philosophy I alluded to earlier, & wonderfully foreshadowed in one of Jerry Rothenberg's famous chants based on Native American materials: "The animals are coming … the animals are coming …" As a useful addition to our last talk, let me mention Donna Haraway. I was listening to her on France Culture, in the program "Les chemins de la philosophie." A whole week was dedicated to her under the title "Donna Haraway, philosophe cyborg." And I thought to myself: "Wow! We speak about the same thing in different ways when I state that purity is the root of all evil." Her idea of the human as cyborg & that we're all connected with different things or realms is exactly that. We're all multiple(s). We're all complex events put together, assemblages, in fact. There is no unity, just as there is no original text.

One other reason I went back to her has to do with some developments in philosophy now that are very important to me. These were brought to me first by Nicole, actually. The woman perspective is always needed to take away our masculine sense of "we know it all" & question our male stance. Nicole, given her love for birds & ornithology, given her efforts to learn about birds, listen to them — better than I because as I get older my hearing becomes a bit weird —, draw them, has birds galore entering her work. Remember we built a canopy with recorded bird songs for our last exhibition in Luxembourg. Thinking about animals became more important to me because of that. She also made me discover the work of Vinciane Despret, a Belgian philosopher based in Liège, who is linked to Donna Haraway. The most interesting thinking happening right now in philosophy, as far as I'm concerned, is interspecies work. Essential to that remains the taking down of the white male as the *summum* of civilization. We have already talked about the great book *The Dawn of Everything: A New History of Humanity*: it does what Haraway, Despret, Olson, & others including myself have been talking about for 30 years, that is the deconstruction of our evolutionary messed up ideology that led to the rather lethal fiction of the white European superman. Something those lazy archaeologists or anthropologists that try to fit new facts into old thinking did not do enough of.

My interest is of course: how can poetry work with this & what is the role of poets in that? I've always maintained since I first read it in 1970 that the poet, as Robert Kelly writes, is "the last scientist of the whole." I cited that in our first conversation in Mersch already! It's that new American poetry when it becomes open field poetry, metaphorically the open space of America — & the world. The poet becomes a generalist, a hunter-gatherer venturing into all the fields, in a way that the hyper-specialist of the 20th century never could. Why did hyper-specialization occur? Because if somebody could find a wider, more integrative angle to look at things, the old myth of some underlying unity would become transparent & demand to be questioned. I still believe that the poet has this cultural role to play. It's of course a very difficult one because of the time it takes to dig into all the fields. But that's why I'm so exalted about *The Dawn of Everything*. They do the job. When I read it, I said to myself: "Yes! You cite the work of Gordon Childe, someone I read already in the late 1960s because of Olson mentioning his work." So the poets — or at least some of them — knew. And with that, I think we're back to where we started out this whole series.

Exactly, & it's really good that after a few rounds we come back to the job of the poet to gather a bit more insight on this very important subject. We've actually been covering various subjects through successive layers of information in different sessions, which is a fine way of getting deeper into important matters, at least in the interview form we chose. And thinking we started today with one specific book & then widened the horizon to all books & all living species, I believe we've been doing the job of the poet pretty well. But let me narrow back to Fox-trails, -tales & -trots for a last quick question. Here's an excerpt of the early fox poems: "cousin / did you ever / spend time / at the emergency / ward, / say, 3 / A.M.? // what struck me / as strange / (the first time) / was that they all / blamed you." I couldn't help thinking about the time the book was published, early into the coronavirus pandemic — I personally read it soon after the first lockdown —, & how much of a coincidence it was (or not?) that these lines were included.

[*Laughs.*] The pandemic didn't come into the construction of the book as it was done before. But that little poem draws on both personal experience & a kind of extrapolation. As a medical student, I would go for a while to hospitals in a *fonction d'externe*, as was said in those days. Remember I also come from a medical family, so my father was called any time of the day or night. In London, I had to go for a couple of reasons to an emergency ward. What I mean there is that people always have an excuse, & the excuse is always someone else. The fox is exactly that figure, in the *Renert* as well of course: he is always blamed for everything bad that happens. The reason he's cunning is that he has to find a way out!

8th & Final Conversation

December 24, 2021

In this last session, I'd like to return to some notions or anecdotes we've already touched upon. One is "the essential between-ness of the world," to quote the title of a recent interview you gave to Nathalie Jacoby in Luxembourg's Tageblatt. Your theater play, The Agony of I.B., *is set in an in-between, & actually this series of talks also, because we're working on a format that is neither strictly a written essay — we work our way through talks — nor a long interview — there is a certain amount of rewriting. We already talked of shamanism, spirits therefore, but somehow I got to think during my preparation, because he, like you, went from Luxembourg to the United States, about the great science fiction publisher Hugo Gernsback. Does the in-between-ness even extend into space?*

Ah! Gernsback … Strange fellow … By sheer coincidence he dies the same month I land in the US, August 1967. Turns out he was a very bad writer but a good entrepreneur & from many accounts a major, if shady, hustler who did much for the field he claims to have invented: science fiction, or "scientifiction," as he preferred to call it. I only really got into science fiction a year later when I shared a house in Rhinebeck with Ken Grimwood during my final year at Bard College — Ken was a total sci-fi, technology, & radio enthusiast & wound up writing a number of novels among which at least one of the greatest fantasy novels of that genre, *Replay*, as well as one of the first major ecologically-conscious novels, *Into the Deep* (1995). Some of the thinking about dolphins that is core to this book had been a major interest of both of us back in the late 1960s, when we devoured John C. Lilly's just published *The Mind of the Dolphin: A Nonhuman Intelligence* (1969). My interest in ecological matter had been raised the previous year when I read Rachel Carson's *Silent Spring* & then by Gary Snyder's various essays in poetry magazines gathered in 1970 in *Earth House Hold*. Ken & I shared a fascination for sensory deprivation tanks, psychedelic underwater adventures, & discoveries in Lilly's work of animal — predominantly dolphin & whale — intelligence & interspecies communication. Now, Ken's medium was prose & mine poetry (oh I wish I had taped some of our night-long discussions on these matters...). Still he got me to catch up with my reading in classical sci-fi, though I'll confess that most of those trad. novels didn't interest me very much, as I saw them as thinly disguised, often weak if not trashy traditional westerns with an uncritical fascination for futuristic technology (rocket planes replace horses, ray- or laser-guns the trusted Colt 45) but with the same white frontiersmen ideology always winning out over differently colored & shaped aggressive "aliens."

Wow! I haven't spoken publicly of my friendship with Ken Grimwood, but now that another Lux-American gave me the occasion, let me slip in a little story: in late 1968 Ken invited me to drive down to Pensacola & his parents' place for Xmas break & I immediately agreed. This was to be my first north-south trip in the US, while the previous year I had done my first east-west trip (New York to L.A.) along Route 66 with friend Stephen Kessler. Two wonderful experiences that got me "on the (Kerouacian) road" which had of course been a major intent when I came to this country. The trip south with Ken also turned out to be adventurous: a pleasant visit of Atlanta & in a brand new high-rise building our first glass elevator "open" to the outside, i.e. not inside a shaft but out against the rising wall — scary & exhilarating, with a slight twist of sci-fi adventure. Then the adventures got more American: the next morning Ken carefully removed the copies of the *New York Times* from the back window of the car as we set out to drive into the Deep South. That night, the motel we had made a reservation at refused to accept us — we realized that our longish "hippie" hair &

budding beards freaked these people out. We drove on to the next town & came up with a routine: Ken had spent a year studying in Paris & spoke French well enough, so we decided to impersonate a duo of French comedians driving to Florida where we supposedly were expected for gigs in Miami — & the con worked, the next motel became deferential, gave us their best suite & asked if we wanted to do a little performance of our routine. We told them we would have loved to but couldn't, bound as we were by contract only to perform in Miami, but maybe on the way back north ... That night we laughed our heads off & headed out toward Pensacola the next morning in excellent spirits — even if on the back roads Ken used to get more swiftly where we were going, those spirits quickly sank, as I grew ever more shocked & dazed by the poverty & open segregation I saw: the small wooden lean-tos & huts just off the road where whole black families lived, children in rags, adults looking away as we drove through. So this was the South — much of it, or rather, those areas where black folks lived, looked like, no, were true economic (& ecological) disaster areas. I had known of this from my readings & the newspapers, but seeing it with my own eyes opened these wider & wider to the racist underbelly of this country.

 Whoops! Now that your one word — Gernsback — has made me spout about 1,000 words, let me turn back to the core of your question, the concept of "the in-between" — even if that one may make me spout several thousand ... You had linked them by asking *"does in-between-ness extend into space?"* I'm tempted to say: it comes from there & has been out there all the time! It's only some of us little *Terriens*, small creatures stuck on Earth, & especially those Northern pale-faces that claim to have founded something they call "Western civilization" (a word Gottfried Benn satirized into "syphilisation") who at one point had the hubris to think that we're all that there is & that we know it all. Or that our reality is the only one & that all that is is somehow one, single, as in one God, as in one truth only, one supreme law, etc. But if you reflect a bit about what humans are actually like, even just physically, anatomically, you start asking yourself why we have or need two eyes to see & two ears to hear — one would be very much enough if there were just one "oneness" out there to be perceived. So there is a complexity in & throughout the world that somehow needs to be put together in order to make it more acceptable as a unity for us, more amenable to our own "understanding" — though if we don't think twice about this we let ourselves easily be fooled into believing in the absolute superiority of the One. We should — & can — know that positing a singular starting point, & then drawing a straight line from there to now, to us, & calling this the natural evolution from some posited low point of origin to a supposed high point that would be us — that's the whole folly of Western civilization saying, "We're it, we're the terminus. There's only one & he looks just like me, a white male." Look, today is the day before Christmas. Tomorrow, we're going to have millions of white baby dolls in cribs, trying to suggest Palestine two thousand years ago. That's insanity. The fact is that we don't see that the world is continuously changing & moving, so that you're always in an in-between.

In your own right, personal history, & dailiness you can locate betweenness: you're constantly twixt sleep & being awake (I nearly said "sleep & wokeness"), a state everybody knows & experiences & that poets & artists often make use of. Images come & you don't know exactly where they come from; as a poet or artist you're really lucky when you can get to the notebook & write them down or draw them. That is the pleasure of poetry also: it makes you write down things you didn't think you had in you & that are from somewhere else. Then you can play & move with them. Using that doubleness of the known & the unknown as you write down what comes from wherever, opens another in-between-ness, inside of which you have not just to be active & work, but you also have to be passive & listen & respond.

So you see, we never left, never will leave betweenness, given that we can't, as that's what there is & where we are. I can't remember exactly the first time I came to the term — & don't have the time to reread myself now — but there is something I haven't talked about much in recent years that has just come to mind. It's an allied or linked term from linguistics, namely the "middle voice." Traditionally in a number of languages there was grammatically a middle voice between the active & the passive modes. You can locate its late avatars, for example in reflexive French verbs like "je m'assois": you do that thing to yourself. It's not "j'assois moi" or "on m'assoit." In Greek, it was a much more visible form. This middle voice seems to have gotten excised from some languages. English in that sense is simplified into just two modes: the active — I kill you — & the passive — I am killed by you. How we lost this middle voice is an interesting question. I don't know if it just fell out of the language or if our own thinking, getting more & more into this ideology of just two things, two modes of action, helped the linguistic shift to happen. But that's a fascinating aspect of language, closely connected to the in-between. For the poet, it's an essential way to proceed to be open to everything. I've always said that it's "both and" & never "either or."

The very notion of in-between-ness collides naturally with what you called earlier the "white male we-know-it-all" attitude. Yet we sometimes need to be grounded in certain convictions. You yourself have been very vocal in the Writers Against Trump *campaign, for example. You also are very active in publishing climate change awareness information on your Facebook page & on your blog, & this theme also comes often into your works. So when does in-between-ness have to give way to action — or does action need a part of in-between-ness to be successful?*

Both-and, again. I don't think in-between-ness means that you sit on the floor between two chairs. You get up. In-betweenness is what makes movement possible by creating space, which allows you to move. *Writers Against Trump* actually comes out of a sense that we're in-between situations & we have to do all we can to influence things. If we know what happened in history, we know that such a situation can go very bad very quickly. So we have to go out & make sure that it doesn't move into that direction. As you know from my writings, I believe we're still in a dangerous place. If I decide that Trump & Trumpism is bad, that's exactly because there is no in-between-ness there! After all, what we hear is: "I know I am right, you're going to shut up or I'm going to make you shut up, whatever it takes." That's fascism, which is the exact negation of any possible thinking in different ways, of actively being part of a world of multiplicities that requires complex thinking.

Now we also know from scientific & pragmatic facts accumulated over the last 60 to 70 years that an ecological disaster is coming at us, or, more accurately, is upon us. If you want, the in-between here could be simply stated: how do we proceed, are there different, multiple ways? There are a range of scientific facts & possibilities of redress, but again it is important to not fall into a simplifying way of thinking that there could be one & only one way of getting out of this trouble. Take the example of one of the major single-solutions proposed: reforestation galore. Excellent when thinking of the deforested areas of the world, North or South, the Amazon basin, say, that were typically heavily forested or rainforest areas. People have calculated the number of trees it would take to replant to tip the balance toward an ecologically positive earth-environment. But in the (comprehensible) haste to find a solution to a pressing problem, those people tend to forget that you can't or shouldn't reforest every possible area. For example, the pine savannas of the US southeast, from Florida to Texas. Although a tree-name is part of that environment's description, it would be a disaster to reforest those savannas with rows of pines. In an excellent article in *Aeon*, the tree-ecologist Francis E. ('Jack') Putz speaks to this in detail, suggesting that "[t]he astounding plant diversity of pine savannas … in their pristine state, [...] would have hosted upwards of 100 species of low-growing understory plants. Included in the understory mix were showy species, like sandhill milkweeds and summer farewell, but also a dozen species of bunch-grasses and sedges, some of which are distinguishable only with magnification. In contrast to that diversity, few species were represented among the scattered trees that overtopped the wildflowers."[9] As always it is the many, not the one, that will prove to be the way(s) to go.

I have an old high school friend in Luxembourg, the brightest kid of my "premiere," who's a retired physics professor, & strangely enough he's a climate change denier. A couple of years ago we had long email exchange, but there was no way of moving him, not even by appealing to his scientific "objectivity" in the face of the accumulated facts. I may have sounded like a one-track mind insisting: "Yes, this is happening." I don't know why I was unable to make an otherwise clear-headed scientist & nature-lover understand what is now obvious to 99% of his community.

But one can still remain in-between & say: "Well, this is what will happen to life forms that are incapable of having a multi-directional relationship with their environment." You can again be in just one place & claim: "Our species is doomed. We're a misconstruction better to be done with, & maybe life will invent forms that are more intelligent." Or you can be in between: "Let's try to see what we can still save from our environment." Last night I went for a walk at sunset & on our 69th Street pier I took a photo of the disappearing sun, then turned 180 degrees & took a photo of Manhattan hit by those last sun rays. I published those two pictures on Facebook, & a friend commented: "From afar, it looks like Utopia." It's totally gorgeous & beautiful, but you also know that a fair amount of the gorgeousness of the sunset may very well be due

9. https://aeon.co/essays/the-tradeoffs-of-savanna-restoration-in-a-tree-crazed-world

to the fact that there are chemicals hanging in the air on the New Jersey horizon where there are many oil & gas depots as well as lots of chemical factories. You have to keep all these things in mind — even when enjoying that gorgeous picture-book-pretty sunset.

There was a lovely park here along the East Side of Manhattan with beautiful trees. In order to protect Manhattan against the rising floods, they decided to cut down the trees to build big concrete dam walls. That was a stupid idea. Obviously, there would have been different ways: it should have been the trees *plus* whatever engineering works were necessary. But we lost that battle: the trees came down last week, & as we drove by the other day we felt deeply saddened. The New York poet Eileen Myles had been very actively working, demonstrating, writing, against that project, as she lives right there in the East Village.

The in-between-ness is a place you need to work from, even if you end up saying that at a given moment in time there is one direction you need to take. But that direction will open up in-between-nesses again & again, because that process evaluation is continuous. There is no final aim; there is only a whole open-ended process, a multi-forked or -pronged network of paths.

So we learned that in-between-ness is a perpetual iteration process, & we'll maybe have to come back to this essential notion in another book, because we'll never be able to exhaust the subject. It was however important to come back today to this notion that was sprinkled throughout almost every other session. Now we talked a lot & in several sessions about epics & how good or bad they can be, about long poems as well. In The Agony of I.B.*, Ingeborg Bachmann says to Hans Werner Henze that she believes she has the right, more, the duty, to "rewrite, write, to compose the myths that we need." The words "we" & "need" are here very interesting: despite having all information at our fingertips, despite the fact that God is dead, why do we still need myths?*

The word "myth" comes from "mouth" in Greek. It is the stories we tell. So we're always at some level in the mythical. We have to rectify the myths told, because of course what happens is that people tell stories to each other, which is fine on a "democratic" level, but once we get in a situation where somebody gets the monopoly — priest, king, president, party leader, whoever — on the story told, that is when the myths get reduced to one myth, you're in a place where you're forced to believe in the one single supposedly "true" version. That's when myth-as-the-story-told congeals into fixed ideology. When I have Ingeborg say that myths are just stories & we can change them, it means that once you find out that the story has been wrong or used in a deleterious way — in that case for half of humanity, to demean women — you retell, rewrite, the story, bring in the other possibilities. It is the job of the poet, the "mythographer" or storyteller, to do exactly that. At this point, retelling the Adam & Eve & the apple is essential, in order to avoid this white male superiority narrative we already touched upon. Rewriting the myth of paradise requires changing those givens.

For me, one of the great heroes in all this, & I don't think we brought him in yet, was Giordano Bruno. He's so wonderfully open-minded, in contrast to nearly all the other monks & priests, as he looked at the world around him — remember he was a trained theologian! — & saw through the myths, in particular the one that has Earth as the center of everything, & began to think in terms of a Galilean universe. That openness & the fact that he was hunted across Europe & ended up briefly in London — where he said something I love quoting, namely that "all science has its origin in translation" — are very important to me. He was burned at the stake in 1600 for believing things that were true, for not buying the frozen myth version of reality that the Church tried to impose. He was an astounding thinker & quite a wonderful poet: if you read the sonnets that run through his philosophical works, they are brilliant. I came across him because in England in 1974–1975

I discovered Frances Yates' book *Giordano Bruno and the Hermetic Tradition*. Bruno was very involved with the various hermetic schools & the magical thinking of that period.

Now, that hermetic tradition is another one exploring the marvelous world of the in-between, take John Dee & his writings in England. Like all mystical traditions, you just can't do away with it & simply disregard it. These traditions explore ways of thinking & traveling in-between, outside of the dogmatics of a given situation, metaphysical or physical. Tarot cards are an incredible, ever-changing universe, because you don't have a fixed beginning or an end; you can read that totally open-ended "book" by shuffling the cards & get completely different takes or tales. That to me is also a very important aspect. I never played much in my work with such chance possibilities, literally, like John Cage, or even closer to me, Jackson Mac Low did, writing poems on cards, so that you could shuffle the poems into randomly determined orders. Jackson also did this as performances where friends/audience members/other poets were invited to pick up a poem-card & read it. To me, it makes complete sense that you can do that. Think about the performance Nicole & I did last July in Luxembourg: some of the texts were nearly randomly chosen & performed by me depending on what Nicole was doing & how I could perceive some things, thus creating other temporary coherences. That is again just traveling this in-between.

The in-between is an open space before all. Take the title of my book *Barzakh*. In Islamic theology that term refers to the period between life & death when the soul travels out of the body & toward its destination; it is often translated as "isthmus," "barrier," "limit" — & theologically seen also as the barrier that keeps the soul from returning to the worldly life. You could also go to Egyptian mythology & see it incarnated as the boat of Ra, while in Tibetan culture it's called the *Bardo Thodol* — literally "Liberation Through Hearing During the Intermediate State" — a guide on how to travel through that interval between death & rebirth. What interests me is of course not some theological interpretation as such, i.e. that you die, get on a boat or some other means of transport, can't turn around & then wind up in heaven or in hell, depending on where the gate-keeper decides to send you. So I would reject the theo-logic of barzakh as barrier, limit, but investigate the term as "isthmus" — which is a strip of land between seas, a place to travel & live on. Borders are never those sharp lines drawn by kings or other authority figures on maps. Actual borders are always porous, traversable, & always constitute areas, isthmuses, eco-niches. Remember that most absolute border in recent European history: the Berlin wall & its continuations. Well, it was not an absolute single line, but a space, an isthmus, with its own ecology of grasses, flowers, rabbits, etc. Where I really saw the coming together of the metaphysical/mystic aspects of that imagination of the in-between with this our daily world & its complexification via the banning of single-line, linear thinking, was in the great Sufi mystic & poet Ibn Arabi's thinking on these matters: when he meditates on the concept of the *barzakh*, he comes to the conclusion that this state of in-betweeness doesn't just describe the state between life & death but in fact is an accurate description of where we all are all the time! That's where we live & move & love & think! It's just the given conditions that we're in. And that's why I called that book *Barzakh*.

That could even be seen as an early scientific article on the conditions of human life.

The concept of the in-between is not just central to poetic imagination; it has indeed become more & more essential to scientific thinking as a way of enlarging our understanding of how things work. We know now that the cosmos is not a billiard table on which balls collide in a Newtonian linear physics of action-reaction, & the biological world of life forms on Terra is not a neo-Darwinian blinkered "struggle for life" where the strongest & best adapted survives, as proposed by that phrase "survival of the fittest." It was back in the early 1970s that my old friend & teacher Eric Mottram explained how that sentence — "survival of the fittest" — was a logical sleight-of-hand, a … what's the term … it's escaping me now … a formal fallacy, in fact, a tautology.

In the years since, so much thinking has been done around these matters, thinking that is brand new & totally relevant to our world today. A vast amount of this thinking & research was & continues to be done by women scientists, & although I already had read some Isabelle Stengers, & back in the 1980's Donna Haraway's *Cyborg Manifesto*, it is only in the last two to three years that I — finally! — came to much of this material thanks to Nicole who, as I mentioned earlier, because of her interests in ornithology, had started to read Vinciane Despret, to who she turned me on, which is leading as we speak to much further reading on & in Haraway, & also in further ecological fields: among others, Anna Tsing's amazing *The Mushroom at the End of the World (On the Possibility of Life in Capitalist Ruins)*, the exploration of an actual present in-between ecology & economy in the North-West of the US, Suzanne Simard's *Finding the Mother-Tree*, which is one of the most radical rethinkings of how life on this planet, in the plant realm, is at its core a matter of mutual aid (interesting at this juncture to reread Peter Kropotkin!) & exchange between individuals of the same species, but also between different species, laying to rest the Über-theory of the "survival of the fittest" individual … while contemplating the ecological disasters the latter theory as employed by foresters in late capitalism has wrought. Or as Lynn Margulis & Dorion Sagan suggested: "Life did not take over the globe by combat, but by networking" (i.e., by cooperation). There is so much amazing work being done right now. I could go one for hours, get Nicole to come & talk too in a collaborative dialogue … & I hope that some of my future projects can bring in, make use a lot of that material &

thinking in the frame of Kelly's "poet as last scientist of the whole" exactly as science is catching up with some of the thinking in the avant-garde arts of the past 100 years — if I may be so bold. It is as if now, at 75, I saw a whole lot of path-breaking thinking, foreshadowed in 20th-century figures such as Olson & Alfred North Whitehead, Robert Duncan's "grand collage," Jerome Rothenberg's "ethnopoetics" & "total translation" experiments, or Muriel Rukeyser's poetry & non-fiction prose & biographies (for when a reprint of her superb *The Traces of Thomas Hariot*?), coming to fruition in not the arts fields, but the fields of science, & not just theoretical science, but applied science. I hope we still have the time to rectify the course of "spaceship Earth," to quote Bucky Fuller.

But to come back to the start of this question, let me expand yet more on the concept of the in-between, in order to suggest that it not only belongs to the arcane spheres of mysticism or of poetics, or even of abstract science, but also to the complex down-to-earth areas of our daily lives in a multicultural world. One such instantiation of "in-betweenness" I came across relatively recently (& spoke to in an interview I gave to The Poetry Project's newsletter & will quote extensively from) was the amazing work done toward a "multicultural" (maybe better the "internal international") poetry going back to, say, someone as radical as Gloria Anzaldúa, who 40 years ago defined herself as a "Shiva, a many-armed and legged body with one foot on brown soil, one on white, one in straight society, one in the gay world, the man's world, the women's, one limb in the literary world, another in the working class, the socialist, and the occult worlds." In that interview I go on to speak of her core concept, Nepantla:

"Anybody writing today, anybody trying to come into a poetry that wants to go deeper than the toxic MFA-mix of identity & confessional, should be familiar with the term and concept she promoted: Nepantla, the Nahuatl word for the in-betweenness, for being in the middle of different things, languages, cultures, etc. As Maria Fránquiz put it: 'The world is in a constant state of Nepantla.'"…

It would be very instructive right now to reread or read for the first time the vast oeuvre of Édouard Glissant, both the poetry and the essays as an insightful correction to over-simplified nationalist identities. Here's a quote: "Fixed identities prove harmful to the sensibilities of contemporary humans involved as they are in a chaos-world and living in creolized societies. A relational identity or a rhizomatic identity, as Gilles Deleuze called it, seems more adapted to the situation. Difficult to admit, but it fills us with anxiety to question the unity of our identity, the hard and unbreachable core of our personhood, an identity closed on itself, afraid of otherness, associated to one language, one nation, one religion, at times to one, race, tribe, clan, one well-defined entity with which one identifies. But we have to change our outlook on identity, as we have to change our relation to the other."[10]

Gloria Anzaldúa wrote brilliantly of what it means & what it can teach us or allow us to learn by living in such a Nepantla, which, let me add, is becoming quickly the normal state of the world: "Living between cultures results in 'seeing' double, first from the perspective of one culture, then from the perspective of another. Seeing from two or more perspectives simultaneously renders those cultures transparent. Removed from that culture's center you glimpse the sea in which you've been immersed but to which you were oblivious, no longer seeing the world the way you were enculturated to see it." Check out her writing & thinking in her (reprinted, 5th edition) *Borderlands — La Frontera: The New Mestiza*,[11] — mapping her experience as a Chicana, a lesbian, an activist, and a writer, in essays and poems profoundly challenging how we think about identity. As the *quatrième de couverture* puts it, her work "remaps our understanding of what a 'border' is, presenting it not as a simple divide between here and there, us and them, but as a psychic, social, & cultural terrain that we inhabit, & that inhabits all of us."

10. *The Poetry Project Newsletter*, Issue #245 (December 2015/January 2016) 19.
11. https://auntlute.com/borderlands

Pierre, we've now reached the very last question of this entire series. But before I ask it, I'd like to remind you, because we won't have time to cover it, that in our second session you mentioned that you had a job as a waiter & sommelier in the Oahu Hilton & that there were great stories attached to it that you'll have to write down at some point. I'm looking forward to reading them in a next book, who knows? Now that this is mentioned: there is a poem by Nicole Brossard to introduce Cartographies of the In-Between, *this book about your work edited by Peter Cockelbergh & which we mentioned several times. In this poem, one can read: "joris iris high risk joy." We talked about poetry, the joy it can & should bring, how essential it is & has always been, but I can't help thinking that the homophony "joris iris high risk" isn't trivial at all here. What is this high risk when it comes to poetry? Or should we understand that the job of the poet is a high risk one?*

I very much think so. The idea that Brossard conveys here in her own words too is that poetry is not that wonderful thing where you remember the great loves of your life & write beautifully about them or a landscape that soothed your broken heart, whatever, & then feel warm-hearted & your mind is put to rest. Another way I talk about this is by mentioning something that Robert Kelly said back in 1967 or 1968 when we were all listening to rock 'n' roll. In a class, he asked: "What do you think the perfect cover for a pop album is?" Nobody said anything, so he answered his own question by: "A mirror!" Because according to RK what you're looking for when you go & experience that kind of music — & by extension, that kind of poetry or art — is self-recognition &, by extension, self-validation. You're saying to yourself: "Oh! That's exactly how I felt when my heart was broken when this girl, this man, or this dog did whatever he/she/it did to me." Then Kelly went on: "Art is exactly the opposite. You follow the art, the poem, the music, whatever & you don't know where it will lead you." That means it's a risky undertaking, because when you go into art, you don't know how you're going to come out. The point of art is to change you. As an experiencer of art, but also as an art maker, you take the very serious risk that your enterprise will change you in some way or other. It may be minimal, but surely you won't, or shouldn't, come out the same person.

So, indeed, the only thing that makes art interesting is that it is risk — in the making & in the perusing of it. For you & for the reader or viewer. If you go to a museum & see all paintings that represent exactly the world as you see it, what would be the need to go there? You just get bored, or maybe reassured that things are what they are. I'd love to be in Paris right now to see these huge paintings by Anselm Kiefer as homages to Paul Celan & his universe. What he does in relation to Celan is risky. I saw his work around Celan & Ingeborg Bachmann six or seven years ago in the Grand Palais already & loved it. Somebody wrote to me asking if I thought Celan would have recognized his Margarethe in the way Kiefer represents her. It's a silly question, because that's not the point. The point of art is to take you to places you haven't been in yet. To make you experience — in mind-body & body-mind — real or imagined scenes, worlds, objects, words, from angles & perspectives you didn't even know existed, & that will have an effect on you, that will change you. By the way, in that sense I understand that some parents will freak out & demand that certain books be banned from the school curriculum, but not because of the use of two "dirty words" or some "communist" suggestions, their superficial/official arguments, but because they know that young people can change inherited ideas, prejudices, etc. after experiencing other ways of seeing & experiencing the world & discovering that that world does not correspond — as they had in fact started to think already — to the pious fixed image projected by parents & guardians of the old order.

Thank you very much Pierre for these hours spent together. That would then conclude the book — unless there is something that I didn't ask & that you're dying to add.

I don't have any conclusive item because that would go against my idea of the openness of things, & maybe when I rework the transcripts I will add & insert things here & there. But I actually want to thank you for the chance to think through all these subjects, because as we were doing this, one thing that came more & more to my mind — & it already started when I did the interviews with Adonis — is that given the times, given my condition, given the fact that I have no more interest in publishing academic essays, what we're doing is working in a relevant in-between genre, like you said at the beginning today. It's the oral & the written, feeding each other, rhythm-ing each other. This I find most interesting, so I am very much looking forward to the book coming out. Maybe we can find another word for "interview." As Rainer J. Hanshe, our publisher, suggests, it could be called "Perceiving between — The science of in-between perceiving." In any case, it's the doubleness & the speed & spin of talking & rewriting. We're in another in-between… as we always are!

Entretien avec Pierre Joris pour *Mélusine au gasoil*

Faut-il être un bon lecteur pour être un bon auteur ?

Oui. Car il faut être à même de bien se lire soi-même pour savoir/entendre/voir si ce qu'on a écrit fonctionne comme on le veut. Même si on lit mal les autres, mais je ne connais pas d'auteur qui ne sache pas bien lire au moins certains autres auteurs. En même temps, être un mauvais lecteur (plus ou moins volontairement, s'entend) pour d'autres peut servir l'auteur.

Même si ton travail de poète comporte une bonne partie d'oralité — lectures ou performances —, tu restes très attaché au livre papier. Qu'est-ce qui motive ta fascination et ton amour pour cet objet ?

Avant l'écriture il y a la lecture. J'ai découvert une vaste partie du monde — le monde visible mais avant tout celui, invisible, de la pensée & de l'imagination — par le livre. Ma bibliothèque m'est indispensable. Et quand je commence à vouloir en faire moi aussi, des livres, je me rends compte qu'avant le livre imprimé il y a les pages du carnet — carnets que j'ai toujours aimé être aussi près d'un vrai livre au niveau de l'épaisseur de la reliure dure, de la taille, etc. —, sauf que les pages sont blanches. Il y a pour moi un immense plaisir sensuel autant qu'intellectuel à écrire à la main sur ces pages vides, jamais avec un bic, objet que je déteste, mais avec un de mes stylos à encre. Sur les années, j'en ai accumulé 18 qui fonctionnent encore aujourd'hui, même si je n'en utilise que 2 ou 3. Un « Aurora Ipsilon Classic » jaune (que Nicole vient de réparer — comme il était tombé et cassé — avec du Gorilla Glue) avec plume F (fine) et de l'encre « American Blue » fabriquée par Private Reserve Ink, et un « Sailor, 1911 Trinity Collection » noir avec plume EF (extrafine) et encre « Jet Black » fabriquée par Diamine. Aurora est une marque italienne et Sailor, malgré son nom, japonaise.

T'arrive-t-il parfois (ou souvent!) de lire tes textes ou ceux des autres à haute voix, même lorsque tu es seul?

Parfois, mais plutôt rarement désormais. Quand j'étais jeune et en phase d'apprentissage et de la langue anglaise et du métier de lecteur/performeur de poésie, je le faisais beaucoup plus. Je le fais encore quand Nicole & moi préparons une performance — en duo, il faut toujours évidemment faire des répétitions (même si on préfère que les musiciens qui se joignent à nous le fassent en impro, donc sans répétitions). Il est vrai par contre aussi que je prépare une lecture publique en lisant les textes du programme que je choisis, pour m'entendre lire ceux que je n'ai pas encore lus en public, mais aussi pour le « timing », pour savoir exactement la longueur de la lecture. Et parfois en écrivant un texte, j'aime bien l'entendre pour voir (hmm, étrange conjoncture des sens dans cette phrase) comment les sons sonnent les uns contre ou avec les autres, et si le rythme des vers fonctionne.

Même si ta poésie et tes essais sont écrits principalement en anglais américain, tu pratiques la traduction de (et même vers) plusieurs autres langues. Chacune d'entre elles est-elle une expérience de lecture différente?

Évidemment — et c'est ça le plaisir du multilingue. Je ne peux m'imaginer ne lire, écrire ou penser que dans une langue — ce serait comme manger tous les jours du poulet-frites : excellent (si bien préparé) en soi, mais après trois jours, y en a marre, faut changer de menu. La même langue pour toute une vie, kifkif.

En plus ces langues différentes se commentent entre elles, se critiquent, voient des choses différentes, se rencontrent au bar pour faire des blagues genre « trois langues entrent dans un bar et le barman leur demande l'autre soir vous étiez toutes ici c'est laquelle qui a oublié sa fourche… », *whatever*, je l'invente sur le tas, mais c'est vrai que mon bonheur c'est d'avoir découvert très jeune que les mots et les choses (*pace*, Michel Foucault) n'ont (presque) rien à voir les uns, les unes avec les autres, à part une certaine, très certaine, musique et la danse effrénée dans laquelle ils se courent les uns derrière les autres et se marchent sur les pieds…

En quoi ton expérience de lecteur s'est-elle modifiée au fil du temps? Comment les technologies numériques l'ont-elles éventuellement influencée?

La vitesse et l'accès. Le numérique a immensément facilité la lecture — mais en même temps il a enlevé un certain confort, *Gemütlichkeit*, peut-être relent petit-bourgeois de la classe qui avait accès (temps et espace) aux livres. Ce nouveau double est un chouia emmerdant car, jeune, j'avais l'arrogante bêtise de croire qu'un jour j'aurai lu tous les livres — je sais maintenant que ce n'est pas ou plus possible, alors pour embêter les autres, je continue d'en rajouter à la Grande Biblio —, mais je préfère encore ceux imprimés sur papier aux fantômes numériques, sauf quand ces derniers sont gratuits et donc accessibles à tous.

Batty Weber Award Speech

Various Variable Words Variably Arranged in the Form of a Celebratory Talk-Essay on Language & Luxembourg on the Occasion of Receiving the 2020 Batty Weber Award

Villmools merci,
    Madame la ministre Sam Tanson
    Madame Fabienne Gilbertz, vice-présidente du jury
    Madame Nathalie Jacoby, directrice du CNL
    & à son prédécesseur, Claude Conter
    & à mon ami Jean Portante

A few months ago as I was thinking about what to say today, I woke up on a hot New York early summer morning just before dawn, the birds already singing, talking, exchanging in the quiet, covid-muted city — I could make out the busy excited chirping of my proletarian house-sparrows (I just learned that North of here they, the sparrows, have changed over the last few years the ending of their song from a series of triplets to a series of doublets — wow! birds create new works too!) and the rarer, sharp, near-metallic chirp of Nicole's favorite, the Northern cardinal.

    From somewhere else an image or a word, a word-image floated much more muted and less dapper into consciousness, arising probably from the dream waking up had made me forget. It coupled two places: Ithaca-Luxembourg/Luxembourg-Ithaca. I knew immediately that Ithaca, NY was not the place that was meant, but that this was Ithaca, Greece. Oh, no, I thought, have I dreamed myself as some kind of modern Odysseus (I always preferred the Greek version of the name to the Latinate Ulysses, probably because I first heard or saw it in German where it is in its Greek version when reading Gustav Schwab's *Die schönsten Sagen des klassischen Altertums* as a kid) (as always parentheses open up when I think or talk or write, and they are often, if not always, about matters of language, of different languages talking to each other — or not), so, as I was saying before I interrupted myself — & thus you too, dear audience, though I won't apologize as this is laying bare the very process of my writing and thinking, so permit me to restart the sentence: Oh, no, I thought, have I dreamed myself as some kind of modern Odysseus returning to Ithaca-Luxembourg after many years of wandering?

No way, José, as we say in New York: I have never been very fond of that founding story of Greco-European culture (even though I enjoyed & learned some from its rewrite by James Joyce in the early 20C), have in fact at times lambasted it as the first bourgeois novel telling the unbelievable and unbelievably macho tale of a warrior who after much slaughter of innocent victims, delayed going home to his quietly and faithfully waiting wife because too busy drinking, carousing, and philandering with various ladies along the road. The gods in the story — "Poseidon made me do it!" — are always a good excuse, here and everywhere else they show up, I mean, we make them up and then have them show up to give us an excuse. That tale finally a glorified epic version of the classic 20C take on the salesman on the road who delays returning to his suburban car, house, son & wife, in that order & for the same reasons. And, maybe most importantly for my own thinking about *poethics* — that's a word I got from the poet Joan Retallack, combining poetry as art, or the art of poetry, "poetics," with the word "ethics" as a moral stance of/in practical living — a word (we're in another language-sandwich parenthesis) that inserts the one sound I still have trouble with after more than half a century in anglo-lands, the english "th" of "the" or "ethics, ethos," & for me worst of all in "though" — though most importantly for my thinking, even if the Odyssey looks like a pre-urban (well, a big city does get destroyed) tale of a man & his friends on the road, it does not speak of a nomadic culture, but defines, requires, insists on a sedentary, (sub)urban one. You go out to return to the same place. A bit more tired but none the wiser?

A few years later I would read much (& translate some) of the French writer Maurice Blanchot's work. In *The Infinite Conversation* he makes the point that what is profoundly non-Greek, i.e. anti-odyssean, in our Judaeo-Grecian heritage, is the figure of Abraham, the settled man of Sumer, who picks up his belongings and leaves, not returning to his (or any One's) supposed origin, but creating his own origin, or as Blanchot puts it: "The origin is a decision; this is the decision of Abraham, separating himself from what is, and affirming himself as a foreigner in order to answer to a foreign truth." It is that relation to alterity or otherness that interests me and which has been central to my incessant movements between countries or what I sometimes call my own micro-continental drifts. To state thus at the outset that beyond any geographical movements, for me, the one place I can find or try to find that relation of alterity is in *poetry*, and the nomadicity of my life is, I hope, replicated (mirrored? better: foreshadowed!) in that of my poetry. It is due to no small extent to what constitutes for a Luxemburger — or at least for me — the greatest plus & simultaneously the greatest obstacle to becoming a writer: the matter of language in the plural. This matter is always present subcutaneously in the poems, sometimes hidden from view as what Ted Berrigan once called "the cheap tricks of the trade," while often flaring up, coming to the surface, becoming the visible topology of the poem itself. Here, an example from *Poasis*, a poem dating to the late 1980s:

MY MOUTH KNOWS A LANGUAGE

my hand & eye cannot imitate,
the mother-tongue there only as *phoné*,
as phoney — though this
    sound-rhyme be phoney
etymology — the fake,
        the counterfeit arising

from Old Irish / Irish Gaelic
    fawney (in which a small
counterfeit deer, or bambi, hides), "a
gilt brassring used by swindlers,"
the book does not
    tell me how
            to use a fawney —
nor if it was a nose ring
    as for cattle
            or a marriage ring
a token of exchange,
or a useless ring except for
    the purported value of its metal
& counterfeit in that?
    So the real root of *phoné*,
sound, voice,
is I-E: bhā̆-, which gives
a list:

fable
fate
infant
preface
prophet
abandon
banish
bandit
fame
phono-
symphony
confess
and (not *and* but)
blame
(end of list)

& while on
American Classics
gravely Jo Cotton
tells the girl with the glycerine tears
"I was a lot of things
a gambler
a thief
a phoney,"
while here
the search goes on, the *phoné*-origins
downloaded days later
searching a CIA database
gathered intelligence
for Luxembourg & got this re ethnic divisions:
    "Celtic base, with French &
German blend."
Like rich coffee,
except whiter,
& the language,
other.

I left Luxembourg in 1965 to go study medicine in Paris. The idea, the expectation — my own somewhat uncertain already, but certainly my parents', my family's, not to say the country's — being that I would return 5, 6, or even 7 years later to become a useful citizen of the upper middle-class medical professions in Luxembourg. It didn't turn out that way — I was never going to live in the country again for more than 3 or 4 weeks at a time at one or more years' intervals. My nomadic life had begun, but looking back on it now more than half a century later, I am happy that it had originated in a small country that was not too heavy — as far as the leaden weight of so many nationalisms with mono-cultural aspirations or impositions are concerned — enabling me to carry it with me wherever I went. As I began to think of my work as nomadic poetry & of a wider nomadic art and existence, one essential description of which is that they must be portable to travel along, I began to see the blessing that a small country like Luxembourg is. So no matter how far away — or out — I went, I would come back more or less regularly, as nomads are wont to do, and I came to see these returns as a kind or resourcing, not just for me resting up in the bosom of the family eating Kachkès, Ham a Judd mat Gardebounen, but for the work too, for the poem, for which it could become a new opening. In the ancient tradition of Arab poetry, the qasida gets its impulse — its opening stanza — from the charge the nomad-poet-traveller experiences when, by chance or by necessity, he or she circles back and comes across last year's camp-fire, the place of origin of the traveling out. In Arab poetics this is called the *atlal*, I'll call it Luxembourg.

This smallness — that, I claimed not just jokingly, makes it portable — paradoxically also entails complexities that many geographically larger countries don't have or claim to have ironed out — the geometry such a space follows is not flatly Euclidian but Riemannian, involving folds upon folds of layers of complexities. One of the core complexities for a writer is of course that of her essential tool, language & the language-folds we are wrapped — I nearly wrote "swaddled" in, like infants, even before language has found us — were and have always remained the richest gift this country could bestow upon me as a writer — even if I was at moments tempted to hear the English word "gift," meaning present, as the German word, "Gift," meaning poison.

I left Paris not only because I had quit medical school to become a writer but because I had decided to write in English — or more accurately in American English. If French or German (& now, Luxembourgish) are the likely languages a Luxemburger normally decides between on the way to becoming a writer, I, except for a very few teenage tries in those languages, always preferred that other one, my fourth language. It is in fact "back home," that is, in the Ettelbruck of my youth, that I discovered the joys of English as American culture was fast becoming the hip space for a teenager to hang out in and aspire to: rock 'n' roll on Radio Luxembourg & various American Forces Networkstations (so much better than the pale imitations in German, say, by Peter Kraus, or in French, say, by fake-American named "Johnny Hallyday"), then Time and Playboy magazines from the Bitburg PX, late-night jazz over AFN & a few other stations (my first published writing was a little essay on Charlie Parker & bebop in the JEC student magazine), & there were blue-jeans or "Texas-boxen" as our parents called them. And, of course, the movies, in the original language with French and Flemish subtitles (the blessings of a multilingual country, ours or the one just to the West: as you couldn't dub a film into only one of the official languages, and as it was too expensive to fabricate two dubbed versions, films got two-languaged subtitles but remained in the original, *en v.o.*): So, innumerable Yankee movies in my grand-mother's now post-Rundstedt restored *Cinéma de la Paix* where once grand-father Joseph had shown Abel Gance's films to himself alone, we all now ate Hollywood from Audie Murphy oaters to James Dean's *Rebel Without a Cause*, while experiencing the ritual WWII "Remembrance Days" with US army participation (Ettelbruck, was also known as "Patton town" for the hero of the Rundstedt whose troops had freed this area from the Germans, shelling the town for days on end and in the process burning my grand-father's large library and correspondence to the ground. I still hold a grudge, and that fact allowed me from early on to reflect critically on military expeditions and adventures). A few years later, on a beach in Spain, a young English honeymooning couple forgot a paperback in the sand, which I picked up: *On the Road* by Jack Kerouac. In the short-lived gay bookshop in the capital, Luxembourg, looking for erotica in Maurice Girodias' green "Traveler's Companion" series, I bought — by mistake (!?) — William Burroughs' *Naked Lunch* and also the City Lights edition of Allen Ginsberg's *Howl*.

But to say that my writing moved between some early poems in German and French and then came to English is already somehow mistaken: years earlier my very first writings happened in totally different languages, or in a language still more radically other: I spent my time scouring Karl May's travel and adventure novels, copying out the Mescalero Apache, Sioux, Comanche, Arab, Persian, Russian, Spanish, American language microliths embedded in the many volumes. From this perfectly heterogeneous language matter copied into an old hard-cover cattle-register my grandmother at the Asselscheuer Haff had given me, I shaped my first writings, which were hero-lists, kinship-lines, tribal schemata, ready-made sentences for explorers and nomadic wanderers, expletives, et cetera. My names were Nikunta, Hadji Halef Omar, Tatanka Yotanka, Gall, Crazy Horse, Winnetou.

But not only literature was a major attraction of that country — another one was its space, and the ensuing kerouacian "on the road," the exhilaration of crossing vast open spaces that reach from ocean to ocean — allowing this European to feel liberated from the weight of history, that swamp in which one is afraid to sink, hip-deep, unable to lift a leg out to move forward, forever hobbled by the weight of the past or condemned to move in deep ruts along a road traced long ago. Yet even when driving fast across the plains you have to stop at some point to eat & sleep or because you meet up with people or do a reading if you are a poet. Some four decades ago, I crossed the US, driving from New York first to Iowa City where I knew I would find a certain poet in a certain bar — you all know him: Nico Helminger! — & from there we drove down to Lawrence, KS & then across the interminable Kansas Plain deep into Colorado.

It wasn't the first time I had done this drive but this time I did it in a rental van, a small U-Haul with many cartons of books in the back. I was moving to California — further away from Luxembourg than I had ever lived. I was elated, but those folds of Riemannian space would catch up with me. Crossing the interminable Kansas High Plains brought back the image of it I had from childhood days in Ettelbruck reading Karl May, dreaming of being a Mescalero Apache called Winnetou and fighting bad white men who came to steal this land, cut it up into largish squares & rectangles & build railroads & roads through it. This was an Ettelbrucker's dream come true — I was driving through Comanche territory. Except there were no Comanche around, none left, the only people here were white descendants of European immigrants. Winnetou had died, or rather Karl May had Winnetou killed, conveniently at age 33, mumbling words about being saved because secretly a Christian. This enraged me back then & enraged me that day driving through Kansas. That night in the motel in Telluride, CO, I prepared a talk & some poems for my reading the next day at a Council of Counterpoetics meeting. I made sure to include sections of WINNETOU OLD, the long poem I wrote in London in the last years before returning to the US. Let me read you a few stanzas of it now:

   staccato stasis howl this alphabet
 go away don't hurl this relapse into bone again
 no gain this stone-monkey Europe post no interglacial basin from its dead foam no Aphrodite no
fat-assed goddess callypigian woman scraggy pigeons of
 Paris Rome London Berlin carriers of Krakow diseases
  kill the messengers from Budapest the plague is
      no turbulence

   breath learn how to breathe with eyes
closed break now the slippery line carry on Winnetou
old now called Taranta in the vision a clearing a oneroom school-house part Swiss chalet part frontier log cabin
part greek temple an old mescalero apache in rags of white
  hair with a ball of light yarn in his right hand

> Itschli dead   he walks in rubber Good Year sandals   the
> light yarn ball raised   his hand raised   all salutes
> resemble each other

That day in Telluride, Colorado, it turned out that there was a Mescalero Apache scholar, Inez Talamantez, among us. Over dinner I asked her about her language, Mescalero Apache, for the preservation of which she worked relentlessly her whole life. I then tried out all the Mescalero words Karl May used in his books — & none of them made any sense to her. It could be that May worked with transcriptions so basic that the transcriber had not realized that Apache was a tone-based language. So May had faked his Indian languages (interestingly, he doesn't do that with Arabic or Persian, the "high cultural," written languages). We went on talking about the problems Apache speakers face today & of the difficulties writing in this & any other Native American language, & thus of the need for native writers & poets to use another than the mother-tongue to write in, English or possibly Spanish, while trying to re-establish, relearn & teach, their own. And all of a sudden I was on familiar territory: the small portable, foldable spaces of multi-lingual needs & possibilities & I realized I had found a *cousinage* in a cultural situation — *toutes proportions gardées* — that had some resonance with my own origins. It is no doubt the questions that such situations raise — but also the richness such territories invariably contain & allow us to discover — that have over the years kept me deeply interested in the ethnopoetic work of Jerome Rothenberg's anthologies, or the explorations of Navajo poets working between their Diné language & English such as Sherwin Bitsui and Orlando White.

    Or, this past week, reading an interview with the Mojave poet Nathalie Diaz whose claim that native languages are "the foundation of the American poetic lexicon" resonates deeply and makes me reflect back on my early years in the US when of course the one great absence was exactly that of Native Americans. Where I live is Lenape land, and "Manhattan" is a Lenape word, just as after crossing the whole continent you will come, as I did, to a peaceful, holy mountain called Mount Tamalpais just North of San Francisco Bay, and if you dig into or under the *word* you discover a Coast Miwok name, *támal pájiṣ*, literally meaning "west hill." Always that eerie feeling when driving across this continent that the native humans have been disappeared, with their traces visible mainly as inscribed into toponyms. Those flat, flat plains are not that flat really; there are folds upon folds of canyons, mesas, arroyos (words from the first colonially imposed language) with toponyms that reach back to & are anchored in the original inhabitants's language. You have to *read* the landscape aloud & *speak* its names to re-aliven its origins. Attention to languages — because as Nathalie Diaz says, "now is an important and dangerous time for language" — is especially necessary in the current political situation, in these not nearly post-covid, Black-Lives-Matter days, as the dangers of pseudo-democratic authoritarianism lurk everywhere.

So it is essential to listen to poets like Nathalie Diaz who, speaking of her people (but, I propose, of all of us), says that "most of us live in a state of impossibility." And then points to a poethics that I find resonates profoundly with my own sense of things, and that is for her, the Native poet, located deep in her language: "In Mojave, our words for want and need are the same — because why would you want what you don't need? For me, that's true desire. Desire isn't frivolous, it's what life is." And it offers a profoundly ecological view of life, digging into which I'll have however to keep for another occasion.

That true desire as the conjunction of want and need, is a complex matter: I have been aware of it ever since I decided to become a writer, something I *wanted* to be more than anything else, and for which I *needed* a language & that was not an easy given. Making the choice — at 19 — to write in my fourth language — a choice I never regretted — has however not either been without moments of anxiety. One of these I tried to catch in a poem from the 70s, which I'll read for you:

ANGUISH, A RIDDLE

>   that all the languages are borrowed
>   but how then do I count them
>   that do not belong to me
>   In the first
>   I think in the second I sink
>   the third is my rhetoric &
>   the fourth my west &
>   wagon its wheel
>   at least traces these steps
>   in harmonies of tetradic modalities
>   before & after I sink

What also helped banish this anguish was the growing realization that writing in one's second, third, or even fourth language is in fact normal. It is only among the conquering European colonial powers — France, England, Spain, even Germany — that the "mother-tongue" has such unparalleled power — probably because its association with "fatherland" creates a Freudian family image that does not want to let strangers in, that wants to keep a mythic purity while functioning as a symbol of imperial-cultural superiority. As a Luxemburger I knew I had to write in a language that was not the mother-tongue (my generation did not even have available the standardized spelling & grammar younger generations have grown up with) while being anguished about the ability of doing so. The poet who brought me to poetry when I was in high school, and who thus in a very real sense set the course of my life's work, Paul Celan, is also the one who states that "only in the mother-tongue can the poet write true poetry — in any other tongue he lies." I am glad that I came across that statement a few years *after* I had decided to write in English & had started to translate Celan into that, this, language — a task I finished just a few months ago, thus after 50-plus years of labor, having now translated his complete poetic oeuvre. I hope I have managed to avoid lies, or at least too many lies, in either my own work or in my translations of his work.

My first engagement with the fact that many writers — besides a few Luxembouregers — write in other than their spoken mother tongues came first in Paris when I met a young Mohammed Khaïr-Eddine, the Moroccan poet of Berber heritage, who told me about the great strength of Maghrebi post-independence writing in French, opening the whole Pandora's box of post-colonial riches & problematics in a range of languages. I would come back to this at a later stage, in the second half of the '70s when I taught at the University of Constantine, in Algeria & was thus able to immerse myself in those literatures. Most of that work has been consigned to & is available in the anthology I gathered with my compadre, the Algerian poet Habib Tengour, a book called *The University of California Book of North African Literature*. It is in these contexts that I learned that the difference between a language and a dialect (& how often has our national language, *Letzeburgesch*, been called just a dialect?) is simply that, as the saying goes, "language is a dialect with guns." It is a matter of political power & cultural independence, of how these two are dependent on each other ("both and," not "either or"), something beautifully stated in the Algerian novelist Kateb Yacine's response to a journalist who after Algeria achieved independence from France in 1962 asked Kateb if he would now write in Arabic, & got this answer: "We won the war so we will keep French as the spoils of war." Languages are portable, portable art. You can take them home.

Demosthenes, as the old story I first heard from my German literature teacher Othon Scholer in the very "classique" Lycée in

Diekirch, held a bunch of pebbles in his mouth to teach himself to speak clearly in public as an orator. May I suggest that the poet, today more than ever, needs to do the same, and learn to speak and write with a bunch of pebble-languages &/or language-pebbles in her mouth. The purity of the single language, as much as of the single culture, not to mention that nefarious fiction, the single "race," is an ideological falsehood, a destructive myth. In my book of essays from the 90s, *A Nomad Poetics*, I insisted that "the only solution" — & I meant in all those areas — "is total miscegenation." I am not exaggerating if I say that again, the atlal of Letzeburg has been helpful for me in coming to this conclusion.

If Hölderlin returned today, Paul Celan wrote, he would only "immerzu lallen und lallen." "Babble" is how I translated Celan's "lallen" in order to be as faithful a translator — & not lie! — as I can be, though I was tempted to use the word "stutter" which poethically may have pointed better to my own understanding of poetry, to explain which I would then have pointed in the commentary to the importance of the stutter, of the act of stuttering in poetry as outlined by Robert Duncan, including to the Demosthenian stutter to be overcome. Or not: stutterless Demosthenian talk too easily becomes smooth discourse meant to seduce, political rhetoric & its flourishes & lies, while the language that stutters remains truer, adhering closer to the essential breath & its turns & twists, & thus to poetry. Then again, my "babble" allows me the echo with Babel, and thus, now, permit me to quote the opening lines of a prose piece that starts in Luxembourg with these lines: "My father was a healer & a hunter. Is it any surprise that I became a poet & a translator? We don't escape our filiations: we only stand more revealed, as the territories shift, as the hunt closes in." This auto-fiction opens my latest book, *Fox-trails, -tales, & -trots*, out last year from Black Fountain Press — thank you, Anne Marie Reuter — who publish books in English here in this country — wow!

I guess there is nothing like words like Babel & babble to make me want to babble or stutter, that is, write on, they, the words, & their amazing histories, which are always multi-lingual, multi-cultural, nomadic in both a vertical, historical, and in a horizontal, geographical, sense, are the poethical materials of my trade. It was Luxembourg's language-bath that started me on these lines of thought, lines that have had me meander through the histories — his-stories, no, her-stories, better, their-our-stories, yes, we have to make the words up if the old ones don't fit any longer! — *and* the geographies of our worlds. And a-babble & a-stutter is how you speak when your language echoes other languages, is other languages, & then you realize that *all* languages are foreign languages, including your mother-tongue. As I learned from the great American poet Robert Kelly, "language is already a second language."

Is there a way to cut through all this language-babble, to set the road straight? My father, the surgeon from Ettelbruck, wielded a jocular but helpful scalpel the day he was pondering the puzzling fact that his son had decided to write in English, and he finally cut through the baloney, saying: "Well, it's not a problem at all really — once you realize that English is just a late dialectical variant of Luxemburgish."

All writing, all poetry, is a trek toward language, our other, the station, the staying in our passage through time. I am a space traveler trying to write myself into an oasis, an amen space as I circumambulate the polis of my life span, stopping here and there. Yet even this station, this *mawqif*, this *poasis* — as I call it with a made-up word or name in the title of one book — is never a given, but always a wrestling so as to expel the slag, burn the dead wood, & rearrange the stones in the ruins of the old camp. To start a new fire to lighten the next steps.

ANTHOLOGIES

The University of California Book of North African Literature (Vol. 4 in the *Poems for the Millennium* series), co-edited with Habib Tengour (UCP, November 2012)

Poems for the Millennium (Vols. 1 & 2), co-edited with Jerome Rothenberg (UCP, 1995 & 1998)

Poésie Internationale: Anthologie (with Jean Portante) (Éditions Guy Binsfeld, 1987)

Matières d'Angleterre (with Paul Buck) (Éditions in'hui, 1984)

EDITED BOOKS

A City Full of Voices: Essays on Robert Kelly, ed. by Pierre Joris with Peter Cockelbergh & Joel Newberger (Contra Mundum Press, 2020)

A Voice Full of Cities: The Collected Essays of Robert Kelly, ed. by Pierre Joris & Peter Cockelbergh (Contra Mundum Press, 2013)

Claude Pélieu: La Crevaille (Posthumous Writings of Claude Pélieu, transcribed & ed. by Pierre Joris) (Ressacs: Éditions de l'Arganier, 2008)

Paul Celan: Selections [Poets for the Millennium series] (University of California Press, 2005)

pppppp: The Selected Writings of Kurt Schwitters (with Jerome Rothenberg) (Temple University Press, 1993; re-issued by Exact Change in 2002)

Joy! Praise! A Festschrift for Jerome Rothenberg on the Occasion of his Sixtieth Birthday (Encinitas: Ta'wil Books & Documents, 1991)

TRANSLATIONS

Mohammed Khaïr-Eddine, *Agadir* (with Jake Syersak) (Dialogos, 2020)

Paul Celan, *Microliths They Are, Little Stones (Posthumous Prose)* (Contra Mundum Press, 2020)

Paul Celan, *Memory Rose into Threshold Speech: The Collected Earlier Poetry* (FSG, 2020)

Safaa Fathy, *Revolution Goes Through Walls* (SplitLevelTexts, 2018)
Marcela Delpastre, *The Blood Stone* (tr. from the Occitan with Nicole Peyrafitte) (Mindmade Books, 2016)
Bernard Manciet, *Ode to James Dean* (tr. from the Occitan with Nicole Peyrafitte) (Mindmade Books, 2014)
Breathturn Into Timestead: The Collected Later Poetry of Paul Celan (FSG, 2013)
Exile is My Trade: A Habib Tengour Reader, ed. & tr. by P.J. (BWP, 2012)
Paul Celan, *The Meridian. Final Version — Drafts — Materials* (Stanford UP, 2011)
Jukebox hydrogène d'Allen Ginsberg (avec Nicole Peyrafitte) (2008)
Paul Celan, *Selections* (UCP, 2005)
Paul Celan, *Lightduress* (Green Integer, 2005)
Pablo Picasso, *The Burial of the Count of Orgaz and Other Writings* (with Jerome Rothenberg) (Exact Change, 2004)
Abdelwahab Meddeb, *The Malady of Islam* (Basic Books, 2003)
4 x 1: Works by Rilke, Tzara, Duprey, & Tengour (Inconundrum Press, 2002)
Paul Celan, *Threadsuns* (Green Integer, 2000)
Michel Bulteau, *Crystals to Aden* (Duration Press, 2000)
Habib Tengour, *The Sandals of Empedocles* (Duration Press, 1999)
Paul Celan, *Breathturn* (sun&moon, 1995)
From the Desert to the Book, Interviews with Edmond Jabès (Station Hill, 1989)
Maurice Blanchot, *The Unavowable Community* (Station Hill, 1988)
Sam Shepard, *Lune faucon* (Christian Bourgois Éditeur, 1987)
Pete Townshend, *Horse's Neck* (Christian Bourgois Éditeur, 1986)
Sam Shepard, *Motel Chronicles* (Christian Bourgois Éditeur, 1985)
Gregory Corso, *Sentiments élégiaques américains* (Christian Bourgois Éditeur, 1977)
Jack Kerouac, *Mexico City Blues* (Christian Bourgois Éditeur, 1977)
Jean-Pierre Duprey, *Temporal Flight* (earthgrip press, 1976)
Julian Beck, *Chants de la Révolution* (Éditions 10/18, 1975)
Carl Solomon, *Contretemps à temps* (Christian Bourgois Éditeur, 1974)

FORTHCOMING

Diwan of Exile: A Pierre Joris Reader (CMP 2023)
Against Tyranny: Selected Essays 1972–2018 (2023)

ON PIERRE JORIS

Pierre Joris: Cartographies of the In-between, ed. by Peter Cockelbergh, with essays on Joris' work by, among others, Mohamed Bennis, Charles Bernstein, Nicole Brossard, Clayton Eshleman, Allen Fisher, Christine Hume, Robert Kelly, Abdelwahab Meddeb, Jennifer Moxley, Jean Portante, Carrie Noland, Alice Notley, Marjorie Perloff & Nicole Peyrafitte (Prague: Charles University, Litteraria Pragensia, 2011)

Samizdat #7, edited by Robert Archambeau (winter 2001): *Rothenberg & Joris: Poets for the Millennium* [https://bit.ly/samizdateditions-issue7]

Oasis #18 (London: Ian Robinson, 1977); new poems by P.J. Essays on P.J. by Eric Mottram, Clayton Eshleman, Robert Kelly. Interview of P.J. by Allen Fisher

ABOUT FLORENT TONIELLO

A Lyonnais for as long as he can remember (1972), an Australian for a year, a Brest & Lille inhabitant during his studies, a Belgian for nearly 15 years with an interval in Amiens, a Luxembourger since 2012, Florent Toniello got lost in the maze of a multinational company that manufactures consumer goods for a long time, mainly in information technology… before meeting poetry.

Since then, he has published poems, short stories or reviews of poetry collections in numerous magazines & anthologies, has written a few books published in Luxembourg, France, & Belgium, & has even had a play performed. He now earns his daily bread from his work as a proofreader & cultural journalist for the Luxembourg weekly woxx, while proofreading novels & poetry collections for several publishers & authors.

Publications include the novel *Ganaha. Un conte futur dans une langue passée* (Jacques Flament, 2020) & the poetry collections *Mélusine au gasoil* (Facteur Galop, 2022), *Vidée vers la mer pleine* (PHI, 2021), *Foutu poète improductif* (Rafael de Surtis, 2018), *Apotropaïque* (PHI, 2018), *L'Oreille arrachée* (maelstrÖm, 2017), *Lorsque je serai chevalier* (Jacques Flament, 2017), *Ptérodactyle en cage* (PHI, 2017), & *Flo[ts]* (PHI, 2015).

ABOUT PIERRE JORIS

Pierre Joris has moved between Europe, the US, & North Africa for 55 years, publishing over 80 books of poetry, essays, trans-lations & anthologies — most recently *Fox-trails, -tales & -trots* (*poems & proses*) (Black Fountain 2020) & the translations *Memory Rose Into Threshold Speech: The Collected Earlier Poetry of Paul Celan* (FSG 2020) & *Microliths They Are, Little Stones: Posthumous Prose of Paul Celan* (CMP 2020). In 2020 he published *A City Full of Voices: Essays on the Work of Robert Kelly* (co-edited with P. Cockelbergh & J. Newberger) (CMP 2020), & earlier, *Arabia (not so) Deserta: Essays on Maghrebi & Mashreqi Writing & Culture* (Spuyten Duyvil, 2019), *Conversations in the Pyrenees* (with Adonis) (CMP 2018), & *The Book of U* (with Nicole Peyrafitte) (*Poems*) (Simoncini 2017).

In 2011 Litteraria Pragensia, Charles University, Prague, published *Pierre Joris: Cartographies of the In-between*, edited by Peter Cockelbergh, with essays on Joris' work by, among others, Mohammed Bennis, Charles Bernstein, Nicole Brossard, Clayton Eshleman, Allen Fisher, Christine Hume, Robert Kelly, Abdelwahab Meddeb, Jennifer Moxley, Jean Portante, Carrie Noland, Alice Notley, Marjorie Perloff & Nicole Peyrafitte. A PDF of his book is available here: https://litterariapragensia.files.wordpress.com/2021/08/cartographies_pierre-joris_peter-cockelbergh.pdf

When not on the road, Joris lives in Bay Ridge, Brooklyn, with his wife, multimedia praticienne & often times collaborator, Nicole Peyrafitte.

COLOPHON

ALWAYS THE MANY, NEVER THE ONE
was handset in InDesign cc.

The text font is *Cormorant*.
The display font is *Halyard Micro*.

Book design & typesetting: Alessandro Segalini

Cover design: Nicole Peyrafitte & CMP
Cover art & photo of Pierre Joris by Nicole Peyrafitte

ALWAYS THE MANY, NEVER THE ONE
is published by Contra Mundum Press.

Contra Mundum Press   New York · London · Melbourne

CONTRA MUNDUM PRESS

Dedicated to the value & the indispensable importance of the individual voice, to works that test the boundaries of thought & experience.

The primary aim of Contra Mundum is to publish translations of writers who in their use of form and style are *à rebours*, or who deviate significantly from more programmatic & spurious forms of experimentation. Such writing attests to the volatile nature of modernism. Our preference is for works that have not yet been translated into English, are out of print, or are poorly translated, for writers whose thinking & æsthetics are in opposition to timely or mainstream currents of thought, value systems, or moralities. We also reprint obscure and out-of-print works we consider significant but which have been forgotten, neglected, or overshadowed.

There are many works of fundamental significance to *Weltliteratur* (& *Weltkultur*) that still remain in relative oblivion, works that alter and disrupt standard circuits of thought — these warrant being encountered by the world at large. It is our aim to render them more visible.

For the complete list of forthcoming publications, please visit our website. To be added to our mailing list, send your name and email address to: info@contramundum.net

Contra Mundum Press
P.O. Box 1326
New York, NY 10276
USA

OTHER CONTRA MUNDUM PRESS TITLES

2012 *Gilgamesh*
Ghérasim Luca, *Self-Shadowing Prey*
Rainer J. Hanshe, *The Abdication*
Walter Jackson Bate, *Negative Capability*
Miklós Szentkuthy, *Marginalia on Casanova*
Fernando Pessoa, *Philosophical Essays*
2013 Elio Petri, *Writings on Cinema & Life*
Friedrich Nietzsche, *The Greek Music Drama*
Richard Foreman, *Plays with Films*
Louis-Auguste Blanqui, *Eternity by the Stars*
Miklós Szentkuthy, *Towards the One & Only Metaphor*
Josef Winkler, *When the Time Comes*
2014 William Wordsworth, *Fragments*
Josef Winkler, *Natura Morta*
Fernando Pessoa, *The Transformation Book*
Emilio Villa, *The Selected Poetry of Emilio Villa*
Robert Kelly, *A Voice Full of Cities*
Pier Paolo Pasolini, *The Divine Mimesis*
Miklós Szentkuthy, *Prae, Vol. 1*
2015 Federico Fellini, *Making a Film*
Robert Musil, *Thought Flights*
Sándor Tar, *Our Street*
Lorand Gaspar, *Earth Absolute*
Josef Winkler, *The Graveyard of Bitter Oranges*
Ferit Edgü, *Noone*
Jean-Jacques Rousseau, *Narcissus*
Ahmad Shamlu, *Born Upon the Dark Spear*
2016 Jean-Luc Godard, *Phrases*
Otto Dix, *Letters, Vol. 1*
Maura Del Serra, *Ladder of Oaths*
Pierre Senges, *The Major Refutation*
Charles Baudelaire, *My Heart Laid Bare & Other Texts*

2017	Joseph Kessel, *Army of Shadows*
	Rainer J. Hanshe & Federico Gori, *Shattering the Muses*
	Gérard Depardieu, *Innocent*
	Claude Mouchard, *Entangled — Papers! — Notes*
2018	Miklós Szentkuthy, *Black Renaissance*
	Adonis & Pierre Joris, *Conversations in the Pyrenees*
2019	Charles Baudelaire, *Belgium Stripped Bare*
	Robert Musil, *Unions*
	Iceberg Slim, *Night Train to Sugar Hill*
	Marquis de Sade, *Aline & Valcour*
2020	*A City Full of Voices: Essays on the Work of Robert Kelly*
	Rédoine Faïd, *Outlaw*
	Carmelo Bene, *I Appeared to the Madonna*
	Paul Celan, *Microliths They Are, Little Stones*
	Bérengère Viennot, *Trumpspeak*
	Zsuzsa Selyem, *It's Raining in Moscow*
	Robert Musil, *Theater Symptoms*
	Dejan Lukiç, *The Oyster* · AGRODOLCE SERIES
	Miklós Szentkuthy, *Chapter on Love*
2021	Charles Baudelaire, *Paris Spleen*
	Marguerite Duras, *The Darkroom*
	Andrew Dickos, *Honor Among Thieves*
	Pierre Senges, *Ahab (Sequels)*
	Carmelo Bene, *Our Lady of the Turks*
	Fernando Pessoa, *Writings on Art & Poetical Theory*
2022	Miklós Szentkuthy, *Prae, Vol. 2*
	Blixa Bargeld, *Europe Crosswise: A Litany*
	Ugo Tognazzi, *The Injester* · AGRODOLCE SERIES

SOME FORTHCOMING TITLES

Kari Hukkila, *The One Thousand & One*
Isidore Isou, *Collected Poems*

THE FUTURE OF KULCHUR
A PATRONAGE PROJECT

LEND CONTRA MUNDUM PRESS (CMP) YOUR SUPPORT

With bookstores and presses around the world struggling to survive, and many actually closing, we are forming this patronage project as a means for establishing a continuous & stable foundation to safeguard our longevity. Through this patronage project we would be able to remain free of having to rely upon government support &/or other official funding bodies, not to speak of their timelines & impositions. It would also free CMP from suffering the vagaries of the publishing industry, as well as the risk of submitting to commercial pressures in order to persist, thereby potentially compromising the integrity of our catalog.

CAN YOU SACRIFICE $10 A WEEK FOR KULCHUR?

For the equivalent of merely 2–3 coffees a week, you can help sustain CMP and contribute to the future of kulchur. To participate in our patronage program we are asking individuals to donate $500 per year, which amounts to $42/month, or $10/week. Larger donations are of course welcome and beneficial. All donations are tax-deductible through our fiscal sponsor Fractured Atlas. If preferred, donations can be made in two installments. We are seeking a minimum of 300 patrons per year and would like for them to commit to giving the above amount for a period of three years.

WHAT WE OFFER

Part tax-deductible donation, part exchange, for your contribution you will receive every CMP book published during the patronage period as well as 20 books from our back catalog. When possible, signed or limited editions of books will be offered as well.

WHAT WILL CMP DO WITH YOUR CONTRIBUTIONS?

Your contribution will help with basic general operating expenses, yearly production expenses (book printing, warehouse & catalog fees, etc.), advertising & outreach, and editorial, proofreading, translation, typography, design and copyright fees. Funds may also be used for participating in book fairs and staging events. Additionally, we hope to rebuild the *Hyperion* section of the website in order to modernize it.

From Pericles to Mæcenas & the Renaissance patrons, it is the magnanimity of such individuals that have helped the arts to flourish. Be a part of helping your kulchur flourish; be a part of history.

HOW

To lend your support & become a patron, please visit the subscription page of our website: contramundum.net/subscription

For any questions, write us at: info@contramundum.net

www.ingramcontent.com/pod-product-compliance
Lightning Source LLC
Chambersburg PA
CBHW031322160426
43196CB00007B/624